AF370469

UNLEASH SECRETS OF LOVE, COMPASSION, AND INTIMATE RELATIONS. SOLUTIONS TO MARRIED LIFE CONFLICTS, BY IMPROVING TRUST, EMPATHY, AND UNDERSTANDING BETWEEN HUSBAND AND WIFE.

Love Your Wife

SOUMITRA SINGH THAKUR

Love Your Wife

Written By: Soumitra Singh Thakur

Published by: Self-Published by Soumitra Singh Thakur

Email: connect@soumitrathakur.com

Website: www.soumitrathakur.com

Address: HN-24, Siddhi Vihar Colony,

Behind - Anjushree Hotel, Ujjain (MP) 456 010

Printed by: Online platforms globally

First published: The year 2020

ISBN: 9 789354 267819

:: Disclaimer ::

This book is a work of nonfiction. Unless otherwise indicated, all the names, characters, businesses, places, events, and incidents in this book are either the product of the author's imagination or used in a fictitious manner. Any resemblance to actual persons, living or dead, or actual events is purely coincidental.

Although the authorpreneur has made every effort to ensure that the information in this book was correct at press time and while this publication is designed to provide accurate information regarding the subject matter covered, the authorpreneur assumes no responsibility for errors, inaccuracies, omissions, or any other inconsistencies herein and hereby disclaim any liability to any party for any loss, damage, or disruption caused by errors or omissions, whether such errors or omissions result from negligence, accident, or any other cause.

Soumitra Singh Thakur is not a spiritual guru, psychologist, or doctor and holds no professional degree, and this should not be considered legal advice. This book does not dispense medical advice or prescribe the use of any statements as a form of treatment for physical, emotional, or medical problems without the advice of a physician, either directly or indirectly. The author intends only to offer general nature information to help you in your quest for emotional and spiritual well-being. The authorpreneur makes no guarantees concerning the level of success you may experience by following the advice and strategies in this book, and you accept the risk that results will differ for each individual. The testimonials and examples provided in this book show exceptional results, which may or may not apply to the reader. They are not intended to represent or guarantee that the reader will achieve the same or similar results. Suppose the reader uses any of the information in this book for himself, as his constitutional right. In that case, the author assumes no responsibility for his actions. If such a level of assistance is required, the services of a competent professional should be sought.

All views expressed in this book are authorpreneur own and do not represent any entity's opinions whatsoever and not necessarily to his employer, organization, committee, or other group or individual with which he has been, and now or will be affiliated.

All of that being said authorpreneur hopes-in all seriousness-that, given the theme of his book and his personal philosophy, the reader can move beyond blame. If anyone disagrees with something, the authorpreneur will welcome a discussion. It would be his privilege to learn from what the reader has to teach him.

This book is dedicated to . . .

The **ether** a universal energy source that is holding and keeping
This planet and all of us; alive in the whole
universe-My Sincere Gratitude to you.
The **Mother Nature** who keeps equilibrium;
Among us without any discrimination. My Sincere Gratitude to you.
My constant energy source and inspiration
Which transmuted me into an enlightened soul in this life
Sant Shiromani Shri Shri 1008 Sagas Baa Sahab Shri Karondia Sarkar
My Infinite Regards and Sincere Gratitude to you.
My Spiritual Guru respected, **Shri Jagdish Chandra Tiwari,**
My Infinite Regards to you.
My Mother, **Mrs. Indu Singh,** with endless regard
Who took all the pains for me to bring me up to this age
and to continue further
My Father, **Mr. Mahendra Singh Thakur,** with endless regard
Who brought me up with all lessons of life
My Love, My Wife, **Mrs. Kokila Singh**
A daring woman who married me and took so much pain in life
To keep me happy and inspired me to write this book.
The title is inspired by her presence in my life, **"Love Your Wife."**
My loving daughters **Joell and Pradnya**
Who taught me to love unconditionally to the world.
My Sweet younger sister **Dr. Shweta,**
To make me learn various life lessons and
remain a constant energy source for me.
My cousin, a genuine cause to write this book; **Mr. Apoorva Bhatt, Kolkata**

And at last but not the least. . .
**To all the men in the world who feel love for
their wives or would-be wives.**

4

Soumitra Singh Thakur

Content

Introduction

Dear, kind-hearted human being.

An avid reader.

A lover of his beautiful wife.

Greetings!!

If, I ask you, DO YOU LOVE YOUR WIFE?

Your obvious answer would be YES.

A Big **YES?**

Well. Who'd dare to say NO?

I haven't met even a single, married man in the 45 years of my life who could declare either publicly or privately that he doesn't love his wife.
WOW!! That's fantastic.
Now. My next question to you is:

Do you really think that all these married men are speaking the truth?

If YES, then the whole world should be in perfect harmony with Mother Nature. Right? All men and women on this planet should undoubtedly be in love with their spouses. There should be No quarrelsome nights. No Separations. No divorce cases. No extramarital affairs. No remarriages. But. Is it so? Tell me. Is it?

Now. I am sure. Your big YES would have turned into a big **No**. And why not?

The truth of loving your wife is an ideal situation that seems to have prevailed during the reigns of an Ideal king and a devoted spouse named "Rama," who lived in the bygone eras of ancient Indian civilizations. In the current times, a dedicated spouse like him adorns only the pages of Indian scriptures. In Fact, in the realms of Indian tradition and culture, words like Divorce and Separation have always been forbidden. Here, marriage is a sacred ritual-an eternal bond. The traditional and ancient cultural practices also depict three significant events in the life of a human being, pre-decided by God even before it takes birth on the earth. They are: "Birth," "Marriage," and "Death." And. In the deepest core of Indian values, people believe that no one can change any of these. However, no one proved it scientifically yet.

People in India marry for a lifetime. They exchange vows to remain together till the end of their lives and also after that. For the next seven births, people believe that marriage keeps bound two hearts, two minds, and two souls. But then God only knows the Truth of reincarnation. Hence, I stick to the Truth of a married man only. So!

What do you think is the Truth of married men?

Well. In my opinion, it is that **"Most"** married men, who claim that they love their wives, actually don't. YES. You read it right. Most men are not happy in their married relationships. They just pretend to be so. And it's great if you don't fall in the **"Most"** category.

Why? Let's try to understand.

Generally, people marry through family arrangements or love affairs or even live-in relationships and enjoy the initial excitement. But the same couple starts feeling suffocated with each other between two to twenty years of togetherness. Some of them even give-in to the rising mental pressures and start seeking separations or other suitable options from the first morning of their married life. In support of my argument, let me just present a reality check in the form of facts and figures in front of you. And. In case you have doubts, help yourself with the vast pool of information available on the internet these days. Here you go!

Divorce/Separation rate in Luxembourg is 87%; Spain 65%, France 55%, Russia 51%, US 46%, Germany 44%, UK & New Zealand 42%, Australia & Canada 38%, and the tragic story continues with many other countries on the list, with various percentages. Here, India stands bottom with 1.5% only. Now tell me, if all men say that they love their wives. WHY is the rate of divorce cases so high all over the world?

Why are there so many family courts, working day in, day out to settle divorce cases among different couples? Why so many specialized Lawyers, Advocates, Marriage Counsellors, and even NGOs are also working in the said direction? Why are there countless relationship self-help books in the market? Many websites on the Internet suggest a thousand different ways of; How to Love Your Wife? Still.

"The Couples are getting separated?" Why?

Do you have an answer to this?

YES...... NO....... MAYBE.

There are extramarital affairs. There are live-in relationships very prominent and getting popular with a rocket speed in society. Suppose you feel that I am putting the facts with exaggerated statements about the institution called marriage. Well. In that case, just try to find your answers. Here I present a few critical QUESTIONS.

What is the number of divorce cases in different parts of the world?

How many celebrities have divorced and remarried so far?

Which is the most expensive divorce case in the world?

What is the number of people living in Live-In relationships in various countries?

Pick up a pen and write your answers in the space given below every question and think. Make an effort. **It's worth !**

The answers will bring the real picture of married men in front of you and help you understand why I made such a **Bold** statement. The statement that **"Most"** men are falsely claiming their love and devotion towards their wives. Also. If, by now, you are finding me somewhat biased towards the men and are wondering why I am not holding the wives responsible for the entire situation. You feel the mess of your life is because of her; that's why you don't love her. There is a list of a thousand irrevocable logics with every man who replies to a family counselor or psychiatrist. Why doesn't he love his wife?

Let me remind you that a man, not a woman, has the privilege of being regarded as the "Head of a family" in most social setups all over the world. Hence, it's you, the man, who has to understand your primary role in the success or failure of a marriage, much before you expect the same from your wife. I know you wouldn't mind holding your wife as the primary suspect of the robbery of happiness caused to your household. You also feel that she has created the entire mess in your life. You have lost all your love and respect for her. But. That is not true. Why? Because you have not only purchased this book but are also reading it. It merely means that you want to discover your faults as well. You haven't lost hope. Either in your wife or the married relationship, you still want to know if you can **LOVE YOUR WIFE.**

ACTIONS SPEAK LOUDER THAN WORDS.

Bravo!

You are a warrior who wants to lose the battle early. Hence. I offer all my help and loyalty as a writer and a devoted husband to YOU. With me, discover such bold facts and insights into your true manly self that you will be left entirely enthralled. Be ready to dive deep into the ocean of a happy married life, that too, in a way that you wouldn't have done so far. Not at least, in your whole married life. Trust me!

Even if you are an eligible bachelor, who wants to love his would-be wife in a way that you would like to bring the MOON and the STARS down on this earth, for her, or would want to take her around for a world tour Or simply hope to shower all the happiness of the world upon her, this book will do wonders for you. But before we do all that, together. Let me just share my innermost intentions behind writing this book with you.

The very idea of writing this book came to my mind when an eligible bachelor who is very close to my heart got married recently.

Apurva Bhatt from Kolkata, a young and dynamic cousin of mine, is just as dear to me as my brother. So! Out of my overwhelming love for him, I decided to give him a memorable gift. A gift for a lifetime. A personal handwritten letter to guide him through the new journey of life. The journey towards a joyous fulfilled married life.

As I sat down to write that particular letter to him, I traveled down my memory lane and started contemplating my own life experiences. While doing that, various memorable moments of my own married life started hovering over my mind. And then, struck a thought of great concern to me. **"Most"** of the married couples these days are not leading happy married lives. Positive and productive emotions like mutual respect, warm intimacy, thoughtful understanding, genuine empathy, loving care, and heartwarming love are dreadfully missing from their relationships. But still, everyone wants to marry. Why? I contemplated further and realized that we all want to have partners for life and live with them happily ever after. It's a calling of the human soul. Hence, it needs to be fulfilled at all costs. That's the point where I decided to shift gears from a long winding personal letter to a self-talk book that will address all issues and concerns related to married life in a detailed manner.

On a superficial level, if we try to figure out a married life's main events, we will understand that every boy becomes an eligible bachelor after attaining a particular age. After getting married, he produces children, indulges in a so-called "fix-timings" job or some other way of earning bread and butter for the family, raises his children, fulfills all their needs, bears all social responsibilities, grows old, and fragile and finally, leaves the world forever. In such a dull, repetitive life. Where does any scope to LOVE YOUR WIFE remain? The answer, I am sure, would be. NONE. But tell me one thing. If given a chance, would you not want to love your wife? If your answer is a big **YES.**

This book, dear readers, is for you.

It will bring many life-saving answers to WHY you should love your wife rather than HOW to do that. Because for a How, I can quickly put forward a few suggestions, such as offering a fresh flower to your wife everyday. Present a surprise gift to her at least once a month. Take her for outings on weekends or go on a long drive with her, with a piece of serene music playing in the background. And yes. Hold her hand and tell her how much you love her after getting up in the morning every day or even before going to bed every night or whenever you get an opportunity. BUT. Let me inform each of you that a **WHY** for anything and everything to prove successful in life comes far earlier than a HOW. Hence, in this book, **I am focusing on WHY you should love your wife.**

This book will talk to you.

Yes, it will!

It is a self-talk book through which you can talk to yourself and answer the questions that arise during the introspection process, take your call and get into the action or correction mode.

Once you face your actual image face-to-face, you will be in a better position to decide how to handle your current situation appropriately. You will agree that there are faults at your end, calling for immediate attention and correction. So, you will start looking for solutions. And you will most definitely get them once you jot them down as answers to the questions that are asked at the end of various phases of life mentioned in the book.

This book will serve as a lifelong practical reference manual for guiding a married man through various growing stages of his married life and prove to be an anecdote for all the eligible bachelors' concerns. Just keep referring to it from time to time and act accordingly. Decide to love your existing or would-be wife from the depth of your heart and be determined to live a joyous married life. And YES.

To ensure success in your endeavors, keep this paperback edition as a reference and a workbook with you. Whenever you feel low in your married relationship, or need some quick guidance, pick up your MAGIC BOOK and go through the particular life phase that you are in at that time. Sit alone. Think far and wide. Talk to yourself, and I am sure you will receive a cure from within. Your inner-self will hold a torch for you, and you will find a way out, most definitely. It will neither judge you nor demean you. But will only expect you to be honest to yourself while answering the mentioned questions. So! Here, they are.

1. Did I get angry with my wife or scolded her even once in the last week?   YES / NO
2. Did I get irritated at any of the points or facts mentioned by my wife?   YES / NO
3. Did I forget what my wife said to bring from the market even once last week?   YES / NO
4. Did I deny any help that she sought for any household chores during the previous week?   YES / NO
5. Did I keep my mobile phone in my safe custody so that she should not touch it?   YES / NO
6. Did I check my wife's mobile phone without her permission anytime during the last week?   YES / NO
7. Did I compare my wife with another woman in the vicinity, in front of her?   YES / NO

8. Do I keep friends with other women without my wife being aware of it? YES / NO

9. Did I speak to any one of them during the last week, in stealth? YES / NO

10. Did I answer all the above questions, honestly? YES / NO

I hope you have tick-marked your honest answers. **NO?** And the last one is **YES.**

Congratulations!

You are an ideal spouse already. So, recall the name of any other married man or even an eligible bachelor who you think deserves this type of thoughtful guidance into leading a joyous married life and give the book to him. **BUT.** If, unfortunately, even two of your answers have a **YES,** there is a dire need for **at least one careful reading of this book** to understand "Why those two answers could not have a NO?"

So, Compassionate humanitarians!

Consider reading this book, a critical mission for leading a joyous and prosperous married life. Summon all your courage and **Take an Oath with me.** Right here. Right now.

I …………………………………………..……………….., (Write your name) swear by the almighty that after having read this MAGIC BOOK from cover to cover, I WILL;

- Understand my wife from a fresh perspective and consider her a worthy human being.
- Give due respect to her and also develop a warm, cozy relationship with her.

- Synchronize my thoughts, feelings, and actions with hers, completely.
- Understand her emotions, background, and expectations from life and me.
- Empathize with her in all the possible ways, as and when required.
- Be truthful, honest to her in the same way I expect her to be with me.
- Take the best care of hers in all the phases of life, good or bad.
- AND. By the end of this book, I will **LOVE MY WIFE** forever.

Done?

If YES, Happy reading to a wife's lover, a handsome man, an intelligent human being, and a faithful husband. Let's start on a cheerful musical note.

Common! **Sing** with me.

"My adorable darling! I think of you... every night... every morning……!!!

Foreword for an Eligible Bachelor and a Married man

"The Only Good Husband, Stays Bachelor: They're Too Considerate
To Get Married."

-Finley Peter Dunne

I think by now, a precipitous curiosity is already brewing up in your mind!!

How will this book serve the purpose of self-talk and a practical reference manual for an eligible bachelor and a married man, simultaneously?

The book will do both. Momentarily, the married man and an eligible bachelor are sailing in the same "Ship." The difference is that the married man is climbing aboard as the first passenger and an eligible bachelor as the last passenger. Both will enjoy the same voyage either enthusiastically or tragically.

After eyeing at the Introduction, you are convinced and confused with two thoughts in your mind. The convincing opinion says; I do agree that there are issues in my married life. Confusing study says that I love my wife, but sometimes I don't. I am confused. Sometimes I like inimical gender too.

You have started thinking. That too, honestly!
Are you curious about how I know that?

Besides having a rich experience in education, I possess a good understanding of human behavior and cognitive processes with practical implementation. Also, having been blessed with a keen sense of observation, I can analyze people vividly and scrutinize the details of human relationships and bonding, even from afar end.

Serving as Principal in school, I put in efforts to reach the root cause of my students' best or worst academic performance in the K-12 segments. The highest factor responsible for students' academic performance is the relationship between their father, mother, and the family atmosphere.

I have observed that students, whose parents have understanding, respect, care, empathy, intimacy, honesty, and love for each other and with their children, are outstanding in academics and co-curricular with higher grades. This theory gave me notable success during my stint as a Principal.

Contrary to this, a quarrelsome, misunderstanding, disrespectful, careless, aloof, dishonest, and without love couple gives birth to several complex issues in the psyche and their children's performance. Such couples mostly have average or below-average performing children. Their grades are primarily low.

To my astonishment, I found even the kindergarten to primary children, who are most observant, in school to their teachers and sometimes to me they say that their father and mother do not love each other. Father scolds mother, and the mother scolds father-my father is a drunk, my father chews tobacco-my father smokes. My mother cries a lot. My parents quarreled yesterday, and my father beat my mother and me. These are very few general statements of students, specifically those who are not performing well. I agree there might be several other aspects to their low performance. Yet, I am trying to bring forth direct or indirect ones related to a couple's strained married relationship. You will be surprised to learn that top performers of my school hardly mention such constraints. Instead, they often praise their parents and show thankfulness towards them for their higher grades.

"The non-performers also hold their parents accountable for not focusing on their studies."

All said and done, and there are always reasons for everything that happens in this world. Therefore, to understand things from a broader perspective, let's first understand a few things about the human mind and its functionalities.

Science proved it. The leagues inform you of psychologists and all the bestseller self-help book authors that the human brain has two physical parts: "The Right Brain" and "The Left Brain." The physical brain has cross-connections of nerves throughout your body. It means that the right brain controls the left part of the body, and the left brain controls the right portion of the body. Also, there are two psychic levels, A "Conscious mind" and a "Subconscious mind." **Isn't it interesting?**

If **YES.** Let me raise your curiosity levels even higher. Generally, we encounter two types of people in our day-to-day life. The first category is of people who think and act from their left-brain. They are logical; their intelligent quotient **(IQ)** is dominant. They put forth logic for everything before reaching the decisions. For rational people, logic is a preference for the cost of human relations during the thinking and decision-making process. Whereas the second category comprises people who think and act from their heart (right brain) (though the heart never thinks, it is a general term to understand). They are emotional and have feelings. They use their right brain. Their emotional quotient **(EQ)** is dominant. They rarely put or value logic; instead, they use their intuition before reaching the decisions. For them, human relations are prominent at the cost of anything, including their life.

As per my knowledge and understanding of human behavior's psychological aspects, disagreements, quarrels or disloyalty, and no love among couples depend primarily upon IQ and EQ. The harmony is considerable; only then will marriage become successful, else not.

It is difficult to understand, so let me try to make it more straightforward and more understandable for you, that too, in a delightful manner. To add a flavor of fiction to your reading enjoyment - I am presenting two characters, "Emuji" for "EQ" and "Iquji" for "IQ." Throughout the book, I will be using these two imaginary characters to refer to the couples they represent. Let me further divide couples into three categories of association.

1st Category: "Iquji" Male and "Iquji" Female

2nd Category: "Emuji" Male and "Emuji" Female

3rd Category: "Iquji" Male and "Emuji" Female or vice versa.

Now. Let me give you a brief overview of thinking and decision-making patterns and identify these people's clues.

The "Iquji" (IQ) males or females males	The "Emuji" (EQ) or females
They think negative more easily than positive.	Have the right side of the brain more active than the

left one. They are excellent organizers in their work.	They might be unorganized but are focused on their wants.
They fail to value genuine relationships, often.	It is challenging for them to understand the logic, especially in emotional situations.
They use their right hand more frequently than the left hand.	They use their left hand more frequently than the right one.
Their conscious mind influences their decision-making process more than the subconscious mind.	They are always near to the people they love.
They focus more on the actual results rather than the process of achieving them.	Most of them have a strong inclination towards the arts.
Everything should take logic, and once they set the logical process to achieve the result, they don't deviate.	They are ready to deviate the set processes to get the desired results.
For them, everything in life is a barter system based on logic, be it business or marriage.	They value human relationships and do not hesitate to sacrifice their interests to save relations.
They find it difficult to understand emotions like love, care, devotion, sacrifice, etc.	They understand and empathize with people from the depth of their hearts.

Generally, there is no disharmony visible in the first and second categories. They understand each other's needs based on the same behavioral pattern and remain in sync, understand, respect, and love each other.

Major issues crop up when there is a match of the third category. Or we can say when Emuji weds Equji. The third category will cover the highest percentage in the pie chart; if researched psychologically. Two individuals who stand poles apart, coming together under one roof, start facing problems, and unfortunately, this category exists worldwide.

Please try to recognize your category. If you realize your type in the beginning only, towards the end, it will be easier for you to evaluate if you are in sync with your wife or not. On confirmation of your type, you will also discover many other things about yourself-even your mistakes. And if you take time to correct them by applying your understanding after reading the book, you will live a joyous married life. Though the success ratio may differ as per the amount of hard work and determination you invest, if you prepare well and implement all the understanding religiously, chances will be very high.

My prime objective is to improve the academic performance of your children, my students. Every parent wants the best grades and a topper in their child. During my remedial strategies, I found an essential family condition always works for the best performing child.

Please be aware that I have used all my knowledge, skills, and practical observations to write this book and have done a lot of careful work in implementing my applicable theories in a trial and error way to get the best result. I found that parents spend a lot of money to get the best academic performance of their children. My

Soumitra Singh Thakur

suggestions do not require a single penny; instead, it will require tremendous effort to put in as a person. A father or a would-be father may experience a constant battle between his mind and heart, between his logic and emotions. His ego, family & economic conditions, peer pressure, society setup, religious values, and many other factors may stop him from following or applying the measures. The individual belief of each person will also create the most significant hindrance on the way. But you will have to stay put on your determination to be a winner in life and not a quitter for your children.

And let me tell you, each of you men can be a winner. Provided the father inside, the man wishes to see his children's best academic and social performance. I hope this objective is sufficient enough to motivate you to follow the corrective measures very honestly. Besides, if you want to transform your house into heaven on earth, this book will serve the purpose for you.

Let me answer one of your more important questions: how do an eligible bachelor and a married man benefit parallelly by reading this book. I have narrated the phases of life in this book, as mentioned in the content. They are from "Preparing to get married" and reaching up to "You alone in your marriage" at last. This book is of utmost help for bachelor and to a man in the previous stage of being alone in his marriage. Each reader needs to associate with the current phase of life and rewind the memoir of his life to the first phase of life. You have to recall all the events of your life which are past now, and once you cross the current stage, you will use this book as a reference manual for the future to get the best results. Eligible bachelors can use it to safeguard from any wrong or negative step in their married life and live a happy life. This book will work for them as a book narrating their future, which they already know, how to improve.

I am narrating a fabricated short story for you to understand why it is essential for you to be a role model.

Let's take an example of a huge manufacturing unit. To run the vast unit, there is tremendous power needed through a big powerhouse. Suppose, due to any reason, this powerhouse stops supplying energy. In that case, irrespective of all machines being new and workable, they won't produce anything. They need the power to run. Now, your family is that vast manufacturing unit. You are a big powerhouse. Suppose you stop supplying energy or divert your energy to the outside, then how will your family; survive ?

If there is a need for refurbishment in the powerhouse, then you have to do that first.

Once the powerhouse is on a regular supply of energy, then only machines can work well. In my next title, **"Love Your Husband,"** the second book of this series, I will talk about the refurbishment of your better half. Suppose you wish that your wife must read the book and improve upon your married life's problems. Before that, you have to be in a constant energy supply. The energy will be available once you apply the book's suggestions with full dedication and devotion.

It is evident that if you cannot make the necessary changes in your behavior and attitude but expect your wife to do the required refurbishment in her life. Then forget about it.

Hello!!

Before changing the world, you have to change yourself.

Suppose you smoke and wish your son must not smoke, then forget

about it. Suppose you drink and hope your son must not drink, then forget about it. Suppose you look to spend time outside of your house with the opposite gender and wish that your wife must not do so, then again, forget about it.

Instead of preaching to your wife to bring the changes or adopt a positive attitude in your married life, you need to change first.

"Be the change first if you wish the world to change for you."

Soumitra Singh Thakur

Before The Beginning of Your Married Life

You are in the twilight zone of your life. The bachelor is about to become a married man. Before the journey of your life, which you are about to enthrall, I must share my inner feeling with all of you about the deep thought on which the whole journey of married life depends.

It would be better to say that the ideology I am about to share with you does not apply to everyone. I could get three types of opinions. My readership will be categorized into three types of readers who would review it as per their idea or thought process or life rules for themselves. First, my brothers would keep my thoughts and get the maximum benefit from this book; second, my brothers may not get along with my thoughts. They may oppose the ideology which I am supporting. Third, my brothers who have not set any rule in their life and they may or may not get along with the thoughts, and they will read the book and decide after that to fix their life ideology to move ahead.

What is the thought which I am presenting through this book?

I support and follow the theory of:

"ONE LIFE ONE WIFE."

You may question me. **Why?**

Being a devotee of spirituality, enlighten, and transmuted personality, in my opinion, the ultimate goal of every human is to achieve salvation in life. Various religions follow different paths to reach the same goal of life. Everyone wants to go to heaven, and no one would ever want to come back from heaven.

You may ask, I mean to say that having one wife in one life is a path to achieve salvation. NO. Kindly do not pretend.

In the materialistic world, everyone who wishes to be a spiritual disciple cannot become a saint and cannot live in Himalaya. We have to live in a society to take care of the family. To learn and become untouched in the materialistic world, we have to limit our wings. The ultimate wish to get along with a spouse is to satiate some desires. Satiating cravings with one or many do make a big difference when we move ahead on the path of enlightenment for our soul.

As per my opinion, if you focus on one wife in one life, you will be able to practice being untouched in the materialistic world. You will learn to live in the present. Your spouse is your present. So! Your zeal to understand the thought will get satiated once you read the book, which will enthrall you.

Read with not your eyes but your heart.

Phase One
Preparing to get married

"Every heart sings a song, incomplete until another heart whispers back.
Those who wish to sing always find a song.
At the touch of a lover, everyone becomes a poet."

- Plato

Wow! Heartiest congratulations!

You are getting married. You got the heart to whisper back for your song to complete it. Let's welcome the fantastic sound and the harmonious rhythm of the marriage. An eligible bachelor is soon becoming a married man. Preparing to get married is the most precious phase in the life of every man. He who gets married and prepares for it remains happy and lives in the present. Some of you are married and reading; you have already enjoyed this phase. You are a responsible man, a loving husband, and the best caring husband of the heart and soul of your better half for the rest of your life, 'Till your last breath,' agree?

The most awaiting phase of your life has arrived since you obtained your adulthood. Before the finalization of your marriage, you might have attended various marriage functions of your cousins, friends, and elders. Your friends must have teased you since your college days about this most important ritual of every male's life. Talking, bullying, and making plans about the marriage or future are vital topics of conversation among bachelors. Suppose I would

29

take examples of this twenty-first-century generation. The cultural traditions are intervening among nations and states. You would understand that the talks and plans for marriage at an early age among boys are not a "Taboo" subject now. Was it a taboo? Yes, in the nineteenth and twentieth centuries, it was. Marriages were not in common to talk before the event.

Why did marriage come into tradition and in practice?

What was the need to get married in society?

Have you thought of, if the man would not have moved into the institution called marriage, what could be society's shape in today's modern era? If the institution called marriage would not have come into existence, then there were no kingdoms built? There was no heir to claim as yours. Suppose there is no heir, for whom anyone would build up the empires. If you know that no one will take care of anything after you depart from the planet earth. (It is about early societal development in ancient civilization). Why would you collect a single penny? You will live your life like an animal. Get up every day, search for food, hunt, eat, mate, and sleep.

There is always a difference between humans and animals. Humans can think. Humans have a conscious and subconscious mind to think and act -the ability bestowed by God, only to humans that they can **THINK** and grow. Early humans have used the power of thinking marvelously and got developed as today's modern individuals. You might think. Why, at the time of my marriage preparation, I am reading about the development of humankind? Let me elucidate it for you.

We have adopted the "Let it be" attitude in our lifestyle during modern individuals' developmental phase. For example, "Edison" made ten thousand failed attempts to get an electric bulb. He was aware of the efforts he put in. So he valued his invention. Today, we do not understand those efforts, and we use electricity with the "Let it be" attitude.

History is full of such inventions and discoveries. May it be the Wheel, Fire, Agriculture, Airplane, Wireless communication, Mobile, Internet, and various day to day activities to make human life comfortable? Humans use everything with a "Let it be" attitude. Likewise. **"Marriage was one of the greatest inventions to make life comfortable and to grow as a society."** That is why up to the nineteenth and twentieth centuries, societies took care of marriages very well. They got nourishments in society throughout the world. Though bigamist, a polygamist culture was persistent in various communities on the family's permission and consent. All the members were living with unanimity in the same family and house. The reasons might be apt as per the period and societal conditions of then, which I am not mentioning here.

What happened now in the twenty-first century is that people do not stay long in marriage? The invention of marriage is the basis of all the development of the world. I mention it "Invention" purposefully. No one discovered it. It was not available in Mother Nature as atoms, molecules, energy sources, and minerals kind of things. The institution "Marriage" got its invention for the sake of societal development. It has proved to be the best invention ever.

Let me explain it to you. **HOW?**

If there was no marriage, it means no woman would stay with you permanently. It means a woman would visit your life as a guest to fulfill the individuals' physical needs and move on. It means a woman would have got pregnant and delivered the baby as per the situation but may or may not be at your place. If there was no marriage, it means there was no home because you have no reason to stay at a place for someone; who is waiting for you. You might have stayed in a group for some time but then got departed searching for a new location or person. If there was no marriage, it means once any of your companion women get pregnant, you would leave her because she won't be in a position for at least twelve months to fulfill your physical demands. So when you have no obligations or emotional attachment with a person. Why would you wait for twelve months? Indeed, you will look for another option because that option would not be objectionable in case of no marriage. There would not be any society in that case. If there was no marriage, it means no family, no relatives, no siblings, no uncle, no aunt, no cousin, and at the top, NO HEIR. In the context of a situation of no marriage, there is no heir in your life. You have no motivation to earn and gather massive wealth.

You always wish that after me, my heir (irrespective of gender) will continue my legacy in this world and grow my name in society. In my opinion, all the developments of communities took place because of this wonderful invention called "Marriage." Marriage motivated the man to construct the house. The man stayed with a woman, called his wife, produced children, and created blood relations. Houses got converted into small villages. In different historical development stages, the small towns got transformed into the modern era's massive cities.

Man safeguarded his wife, his children from all sorts of threats, whether real animals or humans converted into animals. He protected his family because there was a feeling of MINE-My Wife, My Children, My Home, My Village, My Society, My Empire, and My Country.

Anyhow, you **THINK** that, yes, marriage is the greatest of inventions. Great! THEN. Why in the twenty-first-century are marriages moving at a rapid rate towards devastation? It is because humankind has adopted the "Let it be" attitude in marriage. Man has forgotten the emotional pains, physical pains, wishes, expectations, sacrifices, and immolation for the institution called marriage. Man has started thinking that all these are the by-products of marriage. If a woman is marrying, she has to bear all pain. My question to you is: WHY? **THINK.**

In my opinion, marriage is a by-product of emotional & physical pains, sacrifices of hopes & expectations, and lifelong immolation of a woman in her emotional agony. Then you get a successful life under the institution called marriage. A point may arise in your mind that; have women stopped doing all the above for the little wedding. My answer is NO, not at all.

She is still trying her best to endure the emotional & physical pains, sacrifices her hopes & expectations and, immolating her in the emotional fire throughout life. THEN.

WHY ARE MARRIAGES NOT WORKING?

It is because man has forgotten the value of all the above hecatomb of a woman in his life. Man has adopted the easy-go approach. Man has started treating the woman as a product of consumption. (Only by those who fall in the category of **"Most,"** as mentioned in the introduction, and not by all.) A couple's life has become formal and monotonous after getting married. There will be no Love if there is a formality in married life. Love is an abstract feeling which you feel when you are caring for your woman by heart. You value your woman's efforts. You notice that the woman in your life is also a human. She is not a robot. She also, at times, gets tired. She also, at times, needs rest. You will be able to see and become aware of your woman if you value her hecatomb to stay in your life.

You may put up your point that I do take care, and I would care for her throughout my life. I would suggest that this first chapter of the book will be too early to decide whether you take care of her or need a total refurbishment of your heart and mindset or NO.

You are ATTENTIVE by now to love your woman's feelings as soon as you get married or as a mature married man in your married life. I wish to mention that there is a need for **internal preparation** for a successful married life. We prepare externally on a grand level for our marriages. You are for sure preparing for a Givenchy, Gucci, or Raymond's suit, a pair; of Jimmy Choo, Celine, or Ray-ban shades. Various branded accessories for both of you. You are preparing a guest list, making arrangements for delicious foodstuff for the guest. You are making over for your body. You are overhauling your outer appearance with or without clothes.

You and your family are preparing an infinite list of expectations, which no one reveals to the incoming girl in her life. STILL, the list of expectations needs to get fulfilled by your would-be wife, as if she is omniscient. The best thing is that she is not omniscient; still, she also starts acting as if she has the inherent power to read the mind. She will begin putting in efforts to fulfill all the expectations of your family.

What is to be done, THEN?

Prepare yourself from your inner self, along with the outer appearance. Identify and understand that you are **"Iquji"** or **"Emuji,"** and your wife is the opposite of it. Prepare yourself to understand your wife as a human being and not a product to consume. Prepare yourself to understand her emotions and feelings. Prepare yourself to find Love in small acts and CARE for hers. To every wife, little things and considerations matter a lot in comparison to mammoth gifts. Understand that she is not entering into your life to fulfill only the physical desires. You are ready to conquer the battle and come out with triumph. You may think that I don't take her in my life only to fulfill my physical desires. You are right at your place. STILL. Let me clear you. You need to THINK that as per your fantasy, which is the unfulfilled desire.

Typical desires of a male or any eligible bachelor are:

To eat delicious food, you get it from your loving mother. Since your first food feeding, she fulfills all your food wishes, wanted or unwanted, by cooking the most delicious and sumptuous food. You don't need another woman to feed you. You can also hang out with your friends to enjoy the gratifying food.

You may need to get along with the household works for yourself, as making your bed, setting up your closet, taking care of your unorganized kinds of stuff. Again your mother, grandmother, or sister is taking care of. So you don't need another woman to take care of the same.

You may need to travel the world and to different places. Since your inception, your parents and siblings might have arranged various tours to travel. Your childhood friends, adulthood friends are there to hang with you at any place. Your business or office colleagues are there to fulfill all these travel needs. You are always happy with the above members. You are going to enjoy their company forever till your last breath. So you don't need a permanent woman to hang out with for enjoyment.

Then why am I getting married? **THINK.**

There is one desire or wish none of the above people in your life can fulfill. You want to satisfy the physical craving and enjoy parenthood by getting your heir from your wife. For the fulfillment of this desire, the invention of the marriage took place in history. After marriage, once you face the initial tsunami and the moment, water turbulence settles in due time. You start approaching your wife to fulfill only one desire as per your physical need. All other wishes of yours were already getting fulfilled and keep on getting fulfilled forever. May it be your wife or others?

Your wife will satiate your physical desire ONLY, which is the crucial phase in a married couple's life. The moment this phase starts growing in your life, you have to be on alert. **Be cautious;** never let this phase be dominant in your life. You have to be very vigilant for yourself. You have to guard yourself against getting trapped in this situation of life. At this point, **IF YOU COME OUT AS WINNER,** for sure, you are going to ruin your life, AND then you have to be ready to face the repercussions in life.

That this **book is thought-provoking** stuff. It is going to reveal brutal and obnoxious truths about married life. It is not going to present a pleasing picture only. I hope you are ready to move into the most exciting, exuberating, enthusiastic, energetic, charismatic, thrilling phase of your life, THE roller coaster ride of your life. I put my hats off to you from the depth of my heart for fantabulous marriage arrangements.

An eligible bachelor is transmuting into "The Married Man." As this transmutation takes place, I wish that you answer the following questions:

1. Do you agree that marriage has been one of the best

inventions in the history of human civilization?
YES / NO

2.   Do you agree that marriage is a life-changing event for a girl?
YES / NO

3.   Do you realize that there is a need for you to understand the
sacrifices of your better half?
YES / NO

4.   Are you getting married to satiate your physical desires?
YES / NO

5.   Do you wish to convert your house into a living heaven on
earth?
YES / NO

6.   Do you agree that every change flows from the top to the
bottom?
YES / NO

7.   Are you ready to refurbish your inner self?
YES / NO

8.   Do you understand that young kids watch their parents
closely? YES / NO

9.   Have you ever enjoyed any kid mimicking their elders?
YES / NO

10.   Do you agree that you are a role model and a hero to your
kids? YES / NO

Phase Two
The D-Day

"A successful marriage requires falling in love many times, always with the same person."

-Mignon McLaughlin

"What greater thing is there for two human souls than to feel that they are joined for life - to strengthen each other in all labor, to rest on each other in all sorrow, to minister to each other in all pains, to be with each other in silent unspeakable memories at the moment of the last parting!"

-George Eliot

The most awaiting day in the life of an eligible bachelor has finally arrived. The day for you to remember forever in the heart. The day of having lifelong, lively memories in the form of a movie in your mind. The ceremonial rituals may differ, as per the traditions of various communities and nations; one practice is as constant as the Sun. The bride has to leave her house to get married. The groom comes back along with his bride to home after the marriage. All the communities, irrespective of their caste, creed, color, and religion, follow the tradition for ages. It is in our blood-nothing wrong with it.

Then why am I mentioning it here?

I am mentioning to bring an essential fact in your notice that we follow traditions. Even the bride knows since her birth that a day will approach in her life when she will have to leave her home after the wedding. I hope you ever **THINK** that getting ready to leave home is the most significant sacrifice of her life, which she is doing with pride and joy to bring happiness to your life? She left her father, who wiped her tears before they rolled out on her cheeks, a father who fulfilled each of her demands before she made it. Whatever she wished since her birth, her father managed to fulfill her aspiration irrespective of the capacity to spend.

She is leaving her mother, who kept her for nine months in the womb and fed her since she was an egg without becoming an embryo. The mother took all the care of her daughter and never let her face any difficulty in life.

She is leaving her siblings, with whom she played her whole life and grew up. She is leaving her friends of childhood with whom she is comfortable to talk and to share any matter of her life. She is leaving all the known faces, where she has trust; she has faith. She is leaving her house, the known streets, the known worship places, the known vendors of grocery, the known neighborhood.

In short, are you aware that your bride is leaving her comfort zone?

I have a question here: How comfortable are you to come out of your comfort zone in one shot and that too forever?

Give an honest answer to yourself - ....
....

In general, your mother, who came out of her comfort zone years back, will usually never let you move out of your comfort zone. Are you aware of how soon everyone except two people on this planet

forget that the bride has come out of her comfort zone and took the boldest step of her life only to bring happiness to your life? The two persons are your wife and her father; both remember it till their last breath.

You may feel why I am reminding the tradition in such an elaborating way. I wish to bring a fact in your knowledge that in our life whosoever helps us in our tough time, stand with us, hold our hand in need, we always remember that person and remain grateful throughout life. Your better half, who took the boldest step of her life, you never remain thankful to her. Do you **THINK** it is fair enough on your part?

You agree with me that your better half took a bold step, and you must be grateful for her whole life even for this one step. Being a male, you will never be able to take such action in your life alone. I am not referring to you leaving your parental home for the sake of your bread and butter. At that time, your better half will support you, and all your near & dear relatives will be there for your help. In her case, no single person will stand by her. She has to face all her struggles alone.

It is the reason you must say "I Love You" and thank HER forever until your last breath, every morning and every night. You must "Love Your Wife."

Today is the day of your marriage. You have made all the necessary arrangements, and you are ready. You will ride a horse or reach by car to the wedding destination. Your friends, family, and relatives will accompany you. A whole lot of members will accompany you when you are going to marry her. As per the various communities and religious traditions, everyone performs the rituals. All the guests will taste the sumptuous food; they may eat voraciously as a gesture of their presence; this is how customs prevail in the whole world. The approach of functions may differ as per the culture, but the outcome is the same. **I have a question here:**

Why the woman destined to leave the house, and why not, man?

The probable thoughts as per my observations of society come out as solutions are:

Since the early human ages, the Homo sapiens and the following generations felt the family's need. Being the dominant species with a robust and healthy muscular body, the man might have decided to rule the surroundings. Being "Iquji" and following his logic, man always wants to lead his surroundings. In terms of a woman's endurance in the physical and emotional aspects, she is more substantial than a man. Being "Emuji," the woman always gets ready to endure anything at the relationship's cost of preference. Once this fact was in the early society people's knowledge, they should have decided to keep the woman a secondary part. They took the primary role in the family and society. Otherwise, the woman might have superseded the man in the long run in every walk of life till now. Whosoever might have thought of was right in his thought-process.

You got an insight; how a woman has agreed to come out of her comfort zone and left her home to marry. In the long run, women leaving her home became a tradition in society. Everyone forgot about the initial efforts and persistent sacrifices of the woman. Remember that you attend your marriage with so many people. Still, after marriage, when she will come back with you, she always comes alone. On taking such a bold step, she can still be treated well and expect genuine love and care throughout her life. You, being a male, will never win in sacrifices done by a woman for you.

All the rituals got over, and you are officially a married man. Heartfelt congratulations. Exuberant dawn is eager to meet both of you. Birds will sing new songs for you. Soothing breeze and the vermilion sky will welcome you with open arms to take you to the world of love-the ecstasy of life. The most beautiful, splendid journey of your life is called Love. At this point in your life, I wish to give you some thought to ponder about yourself.

Whatever you did or doing from the first step of the bride's finalization, following the marriage date's fixation and all the process between these periods, dominating is you're "Emuji." Although you have an "Iquji" nature, you still adopt a temporary "Emuji" nature. Why? It is because the primary objective is to get married. Your "Iquji" ignores everything. There might be various challenging situations during the marriage, but you overcame them all.

The point is that you took care well. You did not get irritated and did not fall into any tantrums. You handled everything with maturity, understanding, and finally got married. There were various triggering points during the functions of the marriage. You depicted the relaxed, calm behavior and allowed the "Emuji" in you to take charge of your wedding.

I hope you must understand the approach of "Emuji" and "Iquji" in your life. (You can refer to the foreword to understand the "Emuji" and "Iquji" approach to life.) Everyone possesses both. Who is dominating in the given situation is essential. The way you deal under the dominance of "Emuji" or "Iquji" matters a lot in the end. With the practical examples of married life, you will understand this concept well in further reading.

It will be a significant step if you answer the below-mentioned questions to yourself:

1.   Do you agree that there were various challenging situations against your nature during the marriage ceremony, but you handled them with maturity?   YES / NO
2.   Do you agree that you have used your "Emuji" to handle situations at various times?   YES / NO
3.   Do you agree that you preferred human relationships compared to process or logic during your marriage ceremonial functions?   YES / NO
4.   Do you agree that you came out of your comfort zone at various points during your marriage?   YES / NO
5.   Do you agree that you have spent a handsome amount on the maintenance of your outer appearance?   YES / NO
6.   Do you agree that you have made so many plans for a beautiful life along with your wife?   YES / NO
7.   Do you agree that during the marriage, you took utmost care of your; would-be wife?   YES / NO
8.   Do you agree that your wife may possess a nature opposite to you, and she has emotions and feelings for you?   YES / NO
9.   Do you agree that you have made plans enthusiastically for your honeymoon period?   YES / NO
10. Do you agree that you are very eager to explore the world of copulation along with your wife?   YES / NO

Phase Three
The Night of Copulating

"Let there be spaces in your togetherness, And let the winds of the heavens dance between you. Love one another but make not a bond of love: Let it rather be a moving sea between the shores of your souls. Fill each other's cup but drink not from one cup. Give one another of your bread but eat not from the same loaf. Sing and dance together and be joyous, but let each one of you be alone, Even as the strings of a lute are alone though they quiver with the same music. Give your hearts, but not into each other's keeping. For only the hand of Life can contain your hearts. And stand together, yet not too near together: For the pillars of the temple stand apart, And the oak tree and the cypress grow not in each other's shadow."

- Khalil Gibran, The Prophet

The night of the first meeting with your inner-self, the awakening of your desires & fantasies have approached-the first-ever moments of your life where you think that time must stop there forever. The night of having an unrevealed experience in life is with you. The dreams would come true tonight. The most beautiful gift of Mother Nature bestowed to every living creature is with you to experience. HOLD IT. Could you keep it in your memory forever? The same experience would never come back.

Why?

It is because tonight your "Iquji" is sleeping. Your conscious mind is inactive. Tonight you are experiencing all the moments with all the sense of your heart and body. Tonight you are about to reach the destination for a journey that remained very long. Tonight your "Emuji" will be the dominant cause of your involvement. The most important aspect of this whole experience is that tonight the first time, for the entire night you spend in the present time. Tonight is the only night or in any time frame ever of your life, which you would remain in the current time. You will live either in the past or in the future but never in the "Present," after the passing of the night.

How?

Throughout the passing time of tonight, you never think of your past rich or poor experiences. You never think of your economic or financial worries. You never think of societal or peer pressure. You never think of your job security or rise in salary, paying your insurance bills. You do not think of switching jobs, paying debts, finishing a presentation, increasing sales, achieving targets, fearing getting fired or firing someone, parents' health, etc. You also never think of getting a promotion, constructing a big house, and purchasing a Mercedes Benz E-class.

Why?

You are living in the present, the time and moments which are now in your hand. You are conscious that this time will not come back the way it is in your hand or your controls directly. So you want to grab it forever. That is why you wish that time must stop. Time is the most relentless truth of this universe. It never stops.

Do you feel that you are happy because you are going to unfold at an unrevealed destination tonight? Do you think you want to hold the memories of this night because of the satisfaction you will achieve due to the process you are about to involve?

The answer is NO, not at all.

You are happy because you are in the present; you are not thinking anything of the past and not indulging in the future. It is not the process that is making you happy. It is the time, the present time you live in only once in life for tonight. If a function is the cause of happiness, then from now on, you will get involved in the same process for an infinite time. You will never get such satisfaction the way you are satisfied today. Do you think that it is an ambiance or atmosphere responsible for happiness?

You recreate the same or better luxurious ambiance at an exotic location with the same or different partner. It is not the importance of process, place, and partner, which is bringing the experience. You live in the PRESENT, getting a whole new experience in life - this is once a lifetime experience for you. You will never get the inner calmness, serenity, ecstasy, mindfulness the way you are experiencing tonight. All bachelors having this first-ever experience have the option of testing by recreation. You replicate everything whatever you do today for the arrangements the very next night in your life. For sure, you will not experience those moments. Why?

It is because next night you will live in the past and not in the present. All the worries and plans will be there in your mind as your "Iquji" will take charge of your mind. One more critical aspect for you not to live in the present will be that nothing will be explored the next night. You have already unveiled the hidden facts of life. Now it will be repetition. There is no surprise now. Your eyes will not remain wide open. Your jaw will not fall as you might have experienced last night while unveiling each moment one after another. Your "Emuji" was the driving force. Your "Iquji" was sleeping in slumber -This is an essential aspect of living in the present to make "Iquji" sleep in slumber.

THINK that only for one night you spend living in the present gives you such exuberating experiences if you practice living every moment, every night, then how beautiful your life would be with the same spouse forever. Would you be able to think of someone else? IMPOSSIBLE.

All the religious scriptures of each religion, all the saints and priests, spiritual gurus of the current time, philosophers of all the time, motivational speakers, self-help authors putting in their tiresome efforts to make you learn to live in the present time. With their expertise on the subject, they try their best to fulfill this herculean task to make you understand to live in the present and learn to visualize for the future and not worry.

There are two extremely essential factors of your life long memory of tonight and one trivial but necessary element to mention here. The first important factor is that you enjoyed every moment in the present without taking a momentary thought of your past or future worries. The second important factor is that you have unveiled something new today, which you never did, the surprise, the new adventure, the zeal to know the unknown. You have revealed something which you were longing for long. You were dreaming about it for many years. One trivial factor is that if both the partners are losing their virginity tonight, then the experience will remain like a script carved on a stone in your mind and memories.

Now it is an irrefutable truth that you have experienced and tasted the nectar. From now on, the whole life, you will look for this nectar and keep on putting various efforts to test the nectar. You will be investing tremendous efforts to get the nectar next time in life. With the passing night, you forget one critical element out of two,

"Living in the Present," to enjoy the nectar. At the same time, you remember the other essential factor of "Unveiling the Hidden." You will never get the nectar. WHY?

To find the nectar of your life, you keep on sailing the voyage now and then by experimenting with three ingredients. They are process, place, and partner. (Depends on the intensity to get the nectar). In the initial months or years of your married life, you keep changing the process. You consult your so-called maestro friends on the subject. You try to seek help from the internet. This industry has covered seventy percent content sharing to satiate your urge to find the nectar. You try to incorporate the one essential factor of unveiling the hidden. To satisfy this urge, you also put in some of your fantasies based on your reading books related to the topic; available in the market.

The result is you won't get the same nectar that you tasted tonight. One essential factor missing is "Living in the Present." In the next step, you change the place too. The result is the same. At last (but how soon, depends on your zeal to get the nectar), you change the partner. If you are an Indian, then this option is not acceptable in general. In the west, one part of the earth, with the free will society, even this option may be available. The result is the same. You never get the nectar and never stop the search. Suppose you go one step ahead and believe that the pursuit of nectar will get you satiated in heaven, where angels are waiting eagerly for you. You are ready to deteriorate your body to reach heaven early by smoking, drinking alcohol, consuming various drugs. All of us are well aware that this body must be buried or cremated to release the soul to reach heaven. You are doing it hurriedly. You have tried the entire search for nectar here on earth and not finding it. You have tested it once, so you want it at the cost of deterioration of the body. When you consume drugs, alcohol, or indulge in smoking, your brain secretes

Love Your Wife

chemicals like dopamine, and endorphins, which create a fleeting moment for you to live in the present.

Under the impression of all these so-called drugs and other means, you forget the past during the consumption state and never worry about the future. You live in the present. And you have already experienced that living in the present is getting the nectar, so you keep on consuming. The famous Bollywood movie "Sanju" showcased Bollywood giant actor Mr. Sanjay Dutta's real-life story is played by Ranbir Kapoor. It is beautifully picturized that when the actor puts the drug beneath the tongue during the picturesque, the time frame changes. It is like beautiful flowers everywhere, and the experience is like heaven, and everyone wants the same. Drugs and alcohol must be working to aggravate the "Emuji" and subside to the "Iquji" in your mind. Your brain was in the same situation when you were enjoying tonight, tasting the nectar, and living in the present.

You may ask what the point is?

The point is that changing the process, place, or partner will not make any notable change in life, and you won't be able to taste the nectar a second time. The next essential factor in understanding is that you are searching for the nectar outside in the world, which is available there within you. Your eyes are open out, so you are not able to see inside. The key to look inside is to "Live in the Present." To understand how to live in the present, you can regard any current spiritual gurus alive today. The best in the year 2020 is "Sadguru." I can only mention, 'this is the key' and proved to you that you have tested it and enjoyed it tonight.

You may think that you have understood the theory of nectar, living in the present, but how it is beneficial for my married life and love. You are right.

When you know that changing process, place, and partner will not make any difference, stop thinking about adopting this way of finding nectar. Second, you are also well aware that living in the present is the only essential factor. Why not try it? You might have adopted all the means as mentioned earlier, or you may; in the future. You have never tried consciously, purposefully to "Live in the Present." If you plan to live in the present, then there is no harm visible. No liability of lethal effect of drugs or alcohol, no liability of manipulating at home related to erroneous official work, no damage of engaging your mind in making treacherous plans to set the platform to go and try a new process, place, or partner. NO NEED to put passwords in your mobile or laptop and adopt a vigilant and cautious attitude in front of your spouse or close family relations. THINK that if the harms, as mentioned earlier, are not there in your life, then you are already living in heaven without even enjoying the nectar.

Moving further towards the next phase of your life, I wish to clarify the question that I left unanswered above. You will never get the nectar by repeating the same process with the same or different procedure, place, or person. You know that you enjoyed the whole night living in the present. Now on, you will never be in the present because there will be nothing hidden. At the same time, whenever you repeat the same activity, and the moment you reach the peak, you remain in the present for a fraction of a second. Every day you will get to Mount Everest and hardly in seconds come down. The moment of standing on Everest is your moment of the present. The Everest moment will remind you every day, Yes! I am about to test the nectar! And will disappear. The joy, happiness, coolness, and serenity will disappear when you fall from Everest. So this is what the outer world can offer you, nothing less, and nothing more than this. Every day, you go mad in search of tranquility and never get it.

To get this tranquility, you have to turn inside towards your inner self. You have to learn to "Live in the Present," then, while remaining married in life, you will be able to get the nectar from your inside by enjoying this regular process. You can resemble yourself with "Musk Deer," who always seeks for the fragrance, which in reality gets secreted from one of the caudal glands of its body.

Before the dawn approaches, I wish you must answer the questions mentioned here:

1. Do you agree that the copulating night is the only night of your life when you can live in the present? YES / NO
2. Do you agree that living in the present is an essential practice of your life? YES / NO
3. Do you agree that change in process, place, or partner would not bring much difference? YES / NO
4. Do you agree that having an insatiable hunger for a new partner will not lead you anywhere? YES / NO
5. Do you agree that taking the support of alcohol, smoking, or drugs is of no use? YES / NO
6. Do you agree that home will be converted into heaven by your considerable efforts? YES / NO
7. Do you agree that reaching the top of Everest every day will not lead you to get nectar forever? YES / NO
8. Do you agree that there is a need to learn to "Live in the Present" if you wish to have the nectar by remaining in married life and enjoying the same process? YES / NO
9. Do you agree that changes start with yourself? YES / NO
10. Do you agree that every human is like a musk deer? Having nectar inside and not knowing about it. YES / NO

Phase Four
The First Morning

"The most desired gift of love is not diamonds or roses or chocolate. It is focused attention."

- Richard Warren

The dawn has approached. Get up. The new world is waiting for you. The world will meet a conqueror. In the eyes of the world, you are the emperor who holds the crown of triumph. You are the conqueror of the battle of ecstasy. The tragedy of the fight is that one has to lose everything to make the other a winner. The struggle of bliss in which you came as a hero always has a fixed result. The wife has to lose everything to make you the emperor of her life. She makes you the emperor of her heart.

Triumph is always relentless. Here in this battle, her pain is your pleasure. You were unyielding to her last night because her pain was giving you joy. The beautiful fact is that she knows that she has to bear the problem; still, she gets married to you. Being a male, if you are aware that you have to take the pain and lose everything of yours to achieve a purpose in life, you will never do it knowingly. I must say that even destiny is relentless to every woman who bestowed this pain to every girl who takes birth on this planet.

Do you know what she lost? Most importantly, she has lost her virginity. You can think that it is a tradition. I do agree that she did it

Love Your Wife

knowingly. You, as a male, will never dare to do so. The virginity was her ornament till last night. Leave the exceptional cases of today's open-minded society. (That too, only privately, not publicly). Suppose any family and girl announce that she is not a virgin before marriage. You or any so-called modern man will not marry her. So you must value her sacrifice and Love her till your last breath. Say "I Love You" from the depth of your heart, now at this moment when you are reading the book.

The irony of the modern world is that in general (exceptions are acceptable), a man always wants to marry a virgin. The same man wants to lose his virginity (exceptions are allowable) before marriage. Sometimes, God may get confused about where I shall fulfill this demand of the world. How would I supply these many virgin girls for weddings and the same number of girls to make it available for the bachelor to have the beforehand experience?

Next, she has lost her aspirations and ambitions. She might have wanted to conquer the world. She might be a more talented girl than others. She might have got various opportunities in her life. She might have had the ability to be the best sportsperson in the world. She might be a born leader, and if given a chance in administration or politics, she would have done better than others. Tragically she has lost all her aspirations and ambitions for you. It would be best if you respected her abandonment for you, and you must Love Your Wife till your last breath.

Further, she has lost her hope of moving forward in life. She has to stay to support you and carry your family up to the next level to give you an heir. You may think the woman's modern societal setup is standing shoulder to shoulder with the man. Agreed. Tell me one thing. How many times will she start from scratch? Suppose before marriage, and she might have established her own NGO, business startup. Being a professional, she might have set up her office or got a government job. The moment she got married. She has to leave all this in an instantaneous situation. You may counter that she can continue after marriage, agreed. Do you shift your business or job in an instant case? She has to start from scratch at a new place. She does so happily. Within a few years, you want an heir to your family. She is again at zero (exceptions are acceptable). So this is her fate. She has to start from scratch many times if she wants to fulfill her aspirations. It would be best if you regarded her for this abdication of hers and you must Love Your Wife till your last breath.

Additionally, she has lost her comfort zone. In one night, the world has changed for her. You may think that this is how the tradition is, and I do agree. I wish to bring it to your notice because you never thought of it this way. It is not your fault; no one has mentioned you the way I am saying. Till one day before, she was getting up, getting ready as per her comfort. There was no worry about the kitchen for her, as her mother was taking care of it well. She was not worried about any other family member for their tea, breakfast, lunch, or other need. Now, what is the scenario? She has to get-up before you or anyone else. She has to get ready irrespective of her wish or desire. She has to take care of the kitchen and all the members of the family. The overall point is that from now on, she will never be in a comfort zone till her last breath. This dawn, when you are enjoying pleasure, has brought a lifelong tiresome discomfort for her. She accepts it with such joy that you and everyone think that she is the happiest woman by getting married to you. **Admire** her devotion for you and your family and Love Your Wife till your last breath. Here your wife deserves a rose every day. **Show** your gratitude towards her with genuine love.

Lastly, she has lost all her desires. This dawn has brought her a renouncement of desires and wishes. Satire by destiny is that the light which brought contentment in your life has got self-immolation for her. From now on, she will be last to - eat, purchase a new thing, put up a demand, ask for help, seek moral support, and show her tears to anyone in the family. Instead, she will make everyone eat first. Get new materials for everyone. Fulfill everyone's demand, offer help to everyone, provide moral support to everyone, and wipe off every family member's tears till her last breath. **Acclaim** her efforts and Love Your Wife till your last breath. She deserves justifiable care from you as your better half. As a gesture of your love, you must take an oath that you would love her only and not to anyone else. Now, if you say "I Love You" to her, it must be from the depth of your heart and not on the superfluous level.

At this juncture, you may think that she has only lost and got nothing by marrying me. You are right. The thought must strike in your mind. Let's see what she gained today at this dawn.

She has got Expectations. The very first expectation from you is that she must maintain her figure for you and love you only, forever. She should fulfill all your desires and fantasies wanted or unwanted forever. She must cook delicious food for the family. She must remain as young as she is today till her last breath.

She must have got expectations from your mother too, that she should take care of her son and provide an heir to the family as soon as possible. (As if the mother might have forgotten the role of her son in the process). She must be an expert in all the household work the way mother was doing till yesterday. Though the mother might have got expertise in many years, she wishes for an Aladdin lamp to help her daughter-in-law be the expert today. She should be the finest chef, most generous caretaker, preeminent homemaker.

She must have gotten expectations from your father and be a great follower of religious rituals. She should be the best tea maker. She should be omniscient to know when to serve breakfast or lunch, momentarily hunger pops up in your father's stomach. She must be prudent towards his son, i.e., YOU.

In this manner, she acquires the burden of expectations of all the family members. You may put up a point that she has got a loving family. I do agree. You are right. Give one honest thought to yourself; what was wrong with her parents? Did they not love her? Was she not happy at her maternal home? The answer is NO. She was happier. This new family cannot provide her care and love how she was getting at her maternal home. Instead, she has been brought into the family to vouchsafe the fulfillment of expectations of all.

You may put up points on wealth. Your wife has got considerable wealth. Wealth is nothing to do with the girl after marriage. All your materialistic gifts from platinum to airplane are useless if you do not love her and do not care for her. She needs your "Emuji" to handle her, but you think that your "Iquji" will hold her.

It is the most crucial point where you can fall into the trap and start moving in the wrong direction.

Yes, she has got one person in this new home on this dawn today-a person who is the closest to her heart after her father's love. A person to whom; she expects from the core of her heart, the deep love. She hopes that the person will love her as if he loves the virgin queen: the person she got married to a day before, **YOU, the king of her heart.**

You are the only hope for her. You are the expectation, desire, care, and love for her. She needs you in her dismay - this is the reason you must "Love Your Wife."

As we move ahead in the next phase of your life: I wish if you would answer the questions given below honestly for you:

1. Do you feel that you are the conqueror today?   YES / NO
2. Do you feel that she has to lose everything to make you the emperor of her heart?   YES / NO
3. Do you feel that her pain is your pleasure?   YES / NO
4. Do you agree that she has lost her virginity for you? YES / NO
5. Would you ever agree to marry a girl who has lost her virginity before marriage?   YES / NO
6. Do you feel that she has lost her aspirations, expectations, hope, and desires for you?   YES / NO
7. Do you feel that she bears the burden of expectations of you and your family?   YES / NO
8. Do you feel she would be happy if you gave her a platinum ring instead of a loving heart?   YES / NO
9. Do you feel that she can expect at least true love from you? YES / NO
10. Will you "Love Your Wife" forever in a real sense and say "I Love You" with every sunrise and sunset.   YES / NO

I purposefully wish that you must feel and not think in the above questions.

Phase Five
The Honeymoon Period

"Happiness consists of living each day as
if it were the first day of your Honeymoon
and the last day of your vacation."

-Leo Tolstoy

Honeymoon - A Blissful era of your life is waiting for you. In a period, you are about to enjoy the present again. You are at the top of the world. The rhapsody of your life is ready to come out from your inner self. The jubilation of your married life is on the verge of refueling both of you. The euphoria of your life is on the brink of once and forever memoir to both of you. Both of you will laugh in exultation. You are in the vicinity of spending this time rejoicing at your association as a couple. The thrill of your mind and soul will take you beyond the horizon. You will light up with mischievous glee. You are on the threshold of sheerly personal pleasure, which thrives on schadenfreude. Have a pleasant time and make whoopee.

I call the Honeymoon period the gestation time, the incubation period of your married life. The quality of gestation time, the oddity of the incubation period, will decide the fate of your married life. It is all up to you how you spend this duration and what lasting impression it leaves on the mind of both of you individually. My theory for the ideal locus of a victorious honeymoon says: that you must use it as a period of emotional bonding. You have to understand it in ways that suppose you are hurt physically by yourself. You give a settling time to the healing process. Mother Nature has provided a quintessential function of healing for everything in the world. The best in class is "Time."

So! In your opinion, what should be the best utilization of the honeymoon phase?

To understand the utilization of the honeymoon phase, first, you need to understand the inner expectations of both of you individually. Suppose I consider your expectations, as a man, as the dominant species for planning the honeymoon period. In that case, you plan everything by keeping your insatiable physical desire on the primary focus. All your preparation will have physical enjoyment. You will prepare for various places and processes with the same partner. (This is an ideal circumstance that man would have the same partner at least in Honeymoon, irrespective of the number of honeymoons in his life)

Day in and day out, your focus will be on the fulfillment of physical craving. You will visit throughout the world on most exotic locations like; Seychelles: A Land of White Beaches. Hayman Island: The Australian Affair. Kerala: The Finest God's Own Country. Dumfries and Galloway: The Offbeat Scottish Honeymoon. Udaipur: The City of Lakes. Namibia: The Land of Exotic Wildlife. Barcelona: The Charming City of Spain. Las Vegas: What Happens In Vegas Stays In Vegas. Kyoto: The Calmest City of Japan. Cairo: Best of Egypt. Venice: The Romance Capital of Italy. Maldives: The Love Archipelago. Paris: Romance in France. Baja California: Sun-Kissed Beaches. Costa Rica: For Nature Couples, and so on so forth.

What are you going to do in any of the above places? Spend most

60

of your time inside the hotel room, fulfilling all your physical fantasies. You will go to visit all the natural beauty. You will keep your "Iquji" engaged in finding a hiding place in public to satiate your obstreperous physical impulse popping out from you. Once you return, if you sit with your close friend, the one who lives in your heart, and you will share, what did you do? All your sharing will be exaggerated stories of the fulfillment of your erotic enjoyment. You might not remember the beauty of nature. The emotional touches, sunrise beauty, sunset, cool breeze, beautiful, humble, sweet people of the area will not find a place in your memory. You will have the memory of positions where you hid with your beautiful partner to satiate the impulse.

My question is: Is it worth spending a considerable amount as per your pocket size to get the memoir of this value? You can collect a memoir in a local city of residence in a five-star category resort. Satisfy your voracious hunger of having the experience you awaited since you first heard from your friends in a particular age group and since then longing and making plans to achieve it. First, enjoy the fulfillment up to assimilating satisfaction of the hunger. You cannot deny to yourself that you have not made plans. You are not a man in the hunger league. THINK of the facts which will make you realize that you are part of this league only.

First, you are reading this book, reached up to this chapter, enjoying the depiction of the day.

Second, your life achievements are not like Ludwig van Beethoven, The Wright Brothers, Isaac Newton, Dr. APJ Abdul Kalam, Shri Atal Bihari Bajpai, and many more. If you would not have belonged to the league, your name should be on the list of such personalities. Third, it is apt that you have not achieved so far as per the second category people, but you are on the path. I do agree, but then the next area of such work belongs to the field of spirituality. You could have become a priest, a saint, a saga, a guru, or even a spiritual disciple. This book is not fortunate to reach into the hands of the above two category people.

I hope you understood well that you do have hunger; you did make plans for many years. STOP! Misguiding yourself, accept the TRUTH, make your mind, and then read further to "Love Your Wife."

A conscious curiosity must take birth in your mind. How to make use of the precious time of my marriage called "Honeymoon." Yes, now, this is the right way of thinking you have adopted. Moving in the right direction to achieve your goal is covering halfway. As per my theory, the right way to utilize the Honeymoon's precious time is - to have your first Honeymoon in a five or three-star resort of the city for a minimum of ten days. (You only need a clean, hygienic place with availability of food of your choice). Make sure to finalize dates by asking about the moon cycle of your wife's biology. Bring out all your fantasies, satiate all your desires. Forget that there are Sunrise and Sunsets in the world. Get exhausted in such a way that your brain and body must tell you to show mercy. Your mind must apologize to you for keeping you busy making plans for so many years for the Honeymoon. Your brain should stop secreting testosterone chemicals at least for a month. (Ladies, don't worry; I will guide you through handling the situation in my next title, **"Love Your Husband."**)

Your mind will accept that you are fed up with the process, then plan for a real Honeymoon to enjoy.
Choose the best exotic location of your partner's choice. Put your "Iquji" aside and ask your wife. What is her dream location for a Honeymoon?

Stretch your pocket to book the location and squeeze your pocket for the premarital arrangements to showcase. You did marriage for your life and not to showcase the world that suddenly, God bestowed you with the potency today. Investing money in a second Honeymoon will be worth doing ten marriages in one life. Do it and experience it.

The days which you are going to spend will be the golden days of your life. Enjoy the exuberant Sunrise. Grab the energy bestowed by the sky (the ether) on all of us. Listen to the chirping of birds by holding your wife's hand with a smooth touch of your body. Listen to the waves of sea cuddling with your wife, enjoying the wetness and dryness on your body with a compelling combination of waves of water and wind. Taste the sumptuous food of the area served along with the heart full of love by the astounding beautiful people living there. Walk on the streets; experience the love in the eyes of people sitting out of their houses.

Assimilate the innocent smile of kids playing out in the area - it will energize you forever. Explore the beauty of the place; experience the real mountains and valleys in nature instead of coming across them in a hotel room. Feel the beauty of the art and culture of the area. Make local friends, gel along with them, exchange their contacts, and they will keep the memory of a real Honeymoon live forever in your mind. Praise the architecture of the destination and taste the local recipe at your new friend's house. Keep the memory of photographs of this journey in your mind along with the digital one.

Visit the spiritual or religious place of the area as per your religion. Get associated with the spiritual boundary's positive energy and seek lifelong power to receive from the source. This energy will keep both of you in a forever bond and will never let you separate in your life. You are a pure soul. You are an elevated soul. You are a profound soul. You are alive in the present. In this state of persona, the moment you connect with the spiritual energy source, you are bonded forever. Whatever will be the situation in life, this energy source will keep you bonded permanently. (Provided you take a vow; to be so; during getting connected with the energy source.) Message your mind to make your physical hunger to send on vacation after an exhaustive ten days session. Make your wife understand that you have not married her to satiate your physical desire during this Honeymoon. She is far above your physical passion. You care for her. You feel for her. You think of her as a person and not as a body. You touch her the way silk touches her skin.

REMEMBER, every woman seeks a resemblance to her husband. The similarity of a man treated her like a princess since her birth and the growing up stages of her life.

What does a father do? He takes the utmost care of her. Never scolds, never frowns at her. Fulfill her wishes before she makes them. He puts his hand on her head and touches her with the purity of his heart. Always give a positive vibe to her. She feels protected around her father. Every girl looks for a resemblance to her father in her husband. Tomorrow, when you become a father of a cute girl, you will do more than your wife's father did for her.

AGREE or NO?

The state of mind she brought up gets broken when you jump in the bed to satiate your physical desire. That does not mean she is not ready. She is prepared more than you. The way you start; breaks her heart. She surrenders to you the way you want, but you start your life the way she wants. She wants a caring, loving,

Soumitra Singh Thakur

understanding, listening husband. She wants protection in your arms, and you give her a feeling of danger in your arms by your acts. She wants to stay in your heart, and you want to make her sit beneath your heart and belly. The contradiction I am talking about; takes place between you two from your marriage's first night. If given appropriate manure and water, the seeds you sow from the first day of marriage grow into a tree of unbearable fruits within two to twenty years or more in your married life. A day will approach your life to decide not to eat the bitter fruit and cut the tree from the roots. Finally, either you get separated or start looking for another garden to sow the same seed in your life.

My question is:

What is the harm in growing and converting the same tree into the sweet juicy fruits by putting in good manure and atmosphere? You cannot live without eating the fruit. Instead of changing the tree, will it not be better to keep the fruit afresh for every bite. I am not telling you to become her father. That is a metaphor for life. She expects care without anger. She hopes for instructions with love and without scolding. She wants to rest in your lap if she feels tired, the way she sleeps in her father's lap. She hopes that instead of scolding and telling her offensive statements, you let her know about the developments you expect and give time to see the results. She wishes that her husband must maintain equilibrium between her and his family. She hopes that you must inform her well if she commits a mistake or follows an opposite tradition. She expects that her husband must listen and consider her point of view. She wishes that you must consider her opinion during the family's decisions as you call her part of the family. She feels that out of seven days in a week, at least one day, her husband must offer her a cup of tea with love. Even Mother Nature has assigned nine months for a baby to come into the world. Three years of extensive

Love Your Wife

care and nurturing atmosphere for the baby to grow. Fifteen years to become an adult to face the world. You and your family expect your wife to learn your family's traditions, cultures, nature, religious practices, and food eating habits from her mother's womb. As if her mother is omniscient.

Overall she needs your support. Give her. Mother Nature has bestowed her power to convert your house into heaven. She will elevate your generations. You will be proud of her and thank God for sending her into your life. You will thank God for choosing her for you in heaven before your birth. God already did right. You make it wrong on the earth. Do not make a blunder of your life. If you want a Maradona in your home. If you're going to be a proud father of Indira Nooyi. If you wish to have your identity as a father of Sachin Tendulkar, Steve Jobs, Bill Gates, Mark Zuckerberg, Vishwanathan Anand and Serena Williams and many more, than, support your wife.

Think, irrespective of your family situations, whatever person you are today is because of your mother. Your father must have supported your mother. She brought you up. Be grateful to your mother and "Love Your Wife."

To ignite your thoughts, I am putting some questions for you to munch in your mind:
1.   Do you agree that the Honeymoon period is the gestation time for your life long relationship with your wife? YES / NO
2.   Do you agree that you must activate your "Emuji" during the honeymoon period and send "Iquji" to deep slumber?

YES / NO
3.   Do you think that spending money to settle physical hunger via Honeymoon is not the right way to spend the golden moments of life?   YES / NO

4.   Do you think you are the right man to fulfill her expectations
      of being a caring and loving husband?   YES / NO
5.   Do you agree that keeping her sacrifices in mind is justifiable
      that you must "Love Your Wife" forever?   YES / NO

Phase Six
The Pre-Child Phase of Married Life

"Making a decision having a child - It's momentous. It is to decide forever to have your heart go walking around outside of your body."

- Elizabeth Stone

The honeymoon is over. Once in a lifetime, memories are stored in the amygdala via the hippocampus and neocortex. A new life is waiting for you. Your new routine, dreams, visions, and wings on fire to fly. Worries are back. The present is gone, and you are on the ground. The roller coaster ride came to an end, leaving behind forever talks for you to enjoy. You will recall a few joyous moments and few regrets in your loneliness. You got a companion for life in your brain. The moment you feel low, the companion will pop up to help and support you.

Infinite sunrises will be on the way. You will always miss the dawn of the honeymoon. You will love to go back and live again. Time is relentless. You won't get anything in hand except rubbing empty hands. Your empire will not buy you the gone moment. No one can buy a moment. Time is precious.

THINK.

How important is it to live in the present? Learn to live in the present. Start enjoying every passing day with awareness of your actions and words. Be alert for your impulses, actions, reactions, and decisions. Watch your comments before they find a way out of your tongue. Be careful about raising your voice and hands. Cool your frowning eyebrows, train your ears to listen, guide your legs to stroll. Instruct you're mobile not to disturb you during your love moments with your newly married wife.

Now you are thinking. What is the connection between these instructions? I am feeling disconnected. I want you to get disconnected. It is essential to learn - unlearn - and relearn. The above paragraph in italics is a key to successful married life. What do you think?

Expressing that "I Love You" and taking an oath "Love Your Wife" will serve the purpose. Sometimes I think If God must have put in supernatural power in these magical "I Love You" words like the magic mantra of **"Abracadabra."** The world would have become a better charming place. You just say "I Love You," and your part is over. The beauty is that you can speak to anyone and the opposite gender is yours. How beautiful to think? The reality is much more tragic than this magic. You cannot live a contented marriage or love life by narrating "I Love You."

You know: "I Love You" is the cherry on the top of the icing on the cake. Most married men think that putting a cherry on the cake is most important. They can arrange as many cherries as they want. They forget that the delicious cake consists of an actual process of baking a cake. Cake baking has the importance of right temperature (anger), the proportion of ingredients (actions), don't over mix, and don't under mix (words and responses), Bounce back test (thanksgiving), allow cooling completely (apologies), transporting and storing (gratitude).

Did you get any idea? What happened in the above paragraph? You have recently learned to bake the cake of your married life. Is my marriage life a cake?

YES.

Marriage is delicate, like cake baking. The moment you miss one process or ingredient, your cake will spoil. You can enquire with any chef or your wife about the various recipes of delicious dishes. Do you know WHY all the best chef's signature dishes are too expensive?

Is it because the chef is very famous? Do you pay for a chef's name or the taste of a signature dish made by the chef? I pay for the taste of the chef's special.

So, nice of you!

You got the point that we pay for the taste. Then why for a dish the chef charges so high. The chef invests his time, passion, knowledge, and energy to prepare a world-class signature dish to leverage the taste buds, and you are delighted to pay. What is the point of discussing the cake and kitchen? The fact is straightforward, for minuscule satisfaction of your tongue's taste buds, the chef follows a set process. Take care of proportion, time, temperature, ingredients, and above all, remain watchful during preparation. BUT

You do not even pay attention to small acts of yours for the biggest event of your life, i.e., MARRIAGE. You take it so lightly that it ends up one day with each other's separation with escaping velocity. WHY? THINK.

Why do you have a habit of taking things lightly? Do you know the

71

answer?

I am revealing the truth, which you can confirm in your mind.

You take all things lightly, which are readily available to you. Something you do not need to put an effort and they come on your way; sometimes, without putting in many endeavors, you always take them lightly.

Understand this theory from the attitude of humankind towards Mother Nature. Natural resources like water, trees, minerals, oil, coal, and many more in the list are available for humans' use naturally. A common man does not need to put in efforts to get all the resources. He just needs to put some money and get it. He doesn't bother at the time of use. We have used most of the groundwater. We are cutting trees with a speed that trees may be extinct like dinosaurs from the earth in the coming years. You are very well aware that without trees, humankind will not be able to survive. What is your OPINION?

You think that trees will not become extinct until I have my last breath on the earth, so why should I bother. Every generation has felt like this. You start taking care of anything in two conditions. First, either the material is too expensive for you only. Second when you are sure that the availability is at the end and there are no recovery chances. HOW?

Man is the consumer of petroleum available in nature. Mother Nature provided us with oil by processing for billions of years beneath the earth. The traces of the first oil discovery lay from 600 BC to 347 AD. The modern man started using petroleum in its different form in 1859 when Colonel Edwin Drake discovered oil in Pennsylvania by digging a well.

Soumitra Singh Thakur

What is the current status of oil reservoir availability? As per various researches and news flashes in multiple articles, there is a possibility that fossil fuel will end between fifty to a hundred years. My point is not to discuss the fuel getting empty from the earth. My concern is the consumption rate and our attitude towards the awareness and responsibility to take things with their importance in life.

Overall, humans are going to consume all fossil fuel in the next one hundred and fifty years. You calculate total years of consumption from 1859 to 2200 approximately. Humans are about to consume fuel, which took billions of years to be available in just three hundred and fifty years. **It's a big statement.**

People quit smoking when doctors diagnose chronic obstructive pulmonary disease (COPD), including emphysema and chronic bronchitis. People leave alcohol when the doctor diagnoses the symptoms of ARLD depends on the stage of the disease. They may have alcoholic fatty liver, Acute alcoholic hepatitis, Alcoholic cirrhosis. Till this stage, when the government runs various campaigns to make people understand and almost shouts that "Smoking and Drinking is injurious to health," they never quit. Junk food is not nutritious; don't eat. You will have obesity. You will have cholesterol. But no one-stops eating till one of the arteries get blocked. Are you one of those people, THINK

You may ask what connection of all this stuff with my married life when I have just come out of my honeymoon and ready to live a successful married life. You are right. **Just Wait!!**

Have a patient reading, and you will feel that your married life is rocking by understanding all this stuff. Suppose you wish to enjoy the night at home and the noon outside. My apologies to you, sorry:

Love Your Wife

This option is not available from destiny. Then you have to suffer the way many are suffering. Instead, you enjoy every day at home with the same partner and have pleasure every time. Peep Reading this book, and you will discover many secrets for sure.

Also, I am on my way to make you understand the connection of the above stuff with your mind and not with your married life. The problem is in your mind, in your attitude towards things. The way you deal with situations and people decides the result. Suppose I will not put up sufficient examples and would not support my theory with the right life situations. In that case, the recipe will stand half cooked. Do you eat half-cooked dishes? If you are thinking to say, YES. Think two times. You think that I am exaggerating. Okay. Do you believe in experimenting? Experiment with what I am suggesting if you dare to do so?

Tell your wife, newly or experienced, not to cook delicious food, not to make the home, not to make the bed. Let her not keep your clothes in the closet for a month. On an advance note, to test your patience, tell her to sleep in another room for a month. You know Everest will crash. You will go mad. Don't you believe it? Experiment it. Get the proof of all the tantrums which you will create during the period.

Now read with focused attention on the understanding that whatever I am writing here is with the objective that you must remain happy in your life. Once you live happily, then only you will, "Love Your Wife." The moment you love your wife, then both of you will love your children. When you love your children, your children will remain happy. When a child is happy, his/her mind is ready to accept the way information is poured into the mind. So, when your happy child reaches school, the learning will be from the heart, directly registered in the amygdala. The result will be - every student will become the best student.

Now I am continuing to my point that you have a habit of taking things lightly. You take things seriously when they move out of your hands. I put here one more relevant example for you. The moment you get your salary credit, you start spending. Go for a party, shop the latest fashion brand, taste the chef's special dish. Stand in the queue of the apple store to check the latest model. You do the expenditure and come to know by an SMS that you have a ZERO balance in the account. You start complaining about no increment in your salary. The payment is not on time, and the market has a recession; stocks are not showing growth. Next month the same story is repeated. Salary credit. Enjoyment. Blame game.

Have you got my point that you are careless? In the same way, you become most careless about your marriage and married life. **Understand this carefully.**

YOU ARE AT A JUNCTURE OF YOUR LIFE RIGHT NOW AT THIS POINT OF TIME.

How? I am explaining this to you.

You have just finished a memorable honeymoon after a fantabulous marriage function. The last one or two months were fabricated months of your life. It was a show-off game. Don't you believe it? You need examples of everything.

You got your house painted, got a new or refurbished vehicle. You got all your clothes new, including innerwear, a new pair of shoes, the latest fragrance deodorants, and perfumes. You got your hair best in life, with body vexed and toned, with the newest gold or platinum facial.

Be honest and think. Before marriage, did you do all this regularly, say every month or in three to six months! Or you did it for the first time? See, I am talking to the general public. There are exceptional cases in my readership that might be doing righteous things as per need. But the league is minimal in comparison to the general public in the world.

If this was all the first time, then, believe me, it will also be the last time. You won't do it again the way you did in your marriage. What does that mean? It means that you will live a regular life of your own, and the makeup you did at the time of marriage will not be there in your day to day life now.

You and your wife will face each other. You stink, have a foul mouth odor. Your underarms may reveal that you have got an exhaustive day. Sometimes your shoes need to be put outside of the house. You will fart in bed like a child might have touched the chords of a guitar kept in a room. You may drink and come home to bring out the stuff to pour in the sink as if you consumed for the sink. Think that whatever! Whatever comes out of your body in any form, gaseous, liquid, solid, or abstract, it stinks. THINK and then BELIEVE. You can do yourself an experiment by checking the smell. You will smoke and come home, never make your body hair regularly. You would hang out with your friends. Try to keep equilibrium between your wife and your friends & colleagues.

Along with the above realities, you may have some ungentlemanly habit in your day to day life. You pick your nose, scratch your ass, groin either in public or in front of the wife. Spit while talking to someone. You may burp with a drum sound, talking underwater, might have yawned like a Chimpanzee is yawning. You cannot control your leg or hands. They keep on walking while you talk to others. Your eyes are not on the person you talk to; instead, you may stare at various chocolates while conversing. The good thing is that when you indulge yourself in all the stuff, your mind is active in two ways. First, you are entirely unaware. Second, you think no one in the world is watching you, and fun is that everyone laughs at each other. You enjoy kissing your wife after a cloud of smoke or drink. In India and surrounding countries, people have a habit of chewing tobacco. Gosh-awful, horrible; even God will faint at that time.

Do you know your demand for your wife after a drink (if you belong to the category)? You want a copulating session. My sympathies, the poor girl, if she is not a boozer and if she falls into the process, hats-off to her for tolerating hell on this earth. No man can accept the reverse of it even for one time, and she does it for a lifetime. You must say "I Love You" and thank you to her. You will never think of changing in this life. Except for your wife, all the so-called fiancées and your live-in relationship partners will never do it. The moment they become wives, they will do it. The wife should have a very respectful and lovable place in your life. It is the reason that you must "Love Your Wife."

The above three paragraphs are proof that you take things lightly in your married life. Whatever I wrote above is valid only for your wife. The rest of the world will never come to know this naked truth of yours, but only your wife knows. You might be a decent, soft-spoken, well-mannered, formal guy; the world may write a poem on your personality. Your wife knows the liar in you. You watch the audacious and unique act by Jim Carry in the "LIAR LIAR" movie released in the year 1997. You will get a perfect resemblance of my words.

My point here is that the most respected, renounced man of the world will also go naked in front of his wife. Have you ever thought your wife keeps your secrets with such care that you don't even notice? When it is your part to be aware of it and return, she expects a deep intense love in your words and actions. Do you think she is expecting something unthinkable for you? Do you think that giving her a surprise of a diamond to a private airplane and satisfying her in bed will serve Love's purpose? ASK HER?

You will slowly and steadily come out of the wedding hangover in a month or two. Once the hangover is over, both will understand. Oh! It is the reality with which I have to spend my whole life. Some may face an astonishing truth about each other, and a flash of thought may arise. Did I do right by marrying this person?

All this process will be everyday routine life for you, about the honeymoon depending on your nature, how you have enjoyed it. Suppose you wish to enjoy the showers of rain without an umbrella or a raincoat. The opposite is also true: you may enjoy rain showers using an umbrella or a raincoat. The way of enjoyment of rain will decide whether you are going to become a proud father of your baby in the next nine months or not.

The good news may be on the way for you at any time by now.

By the time you wait for the goosebumps in your body on the magical words by your doctor. Bravo!! You are going to become a father. I take you through the thought process so that, along with the triumphant state of mind, you also keep on thinking about the best married life.

1. Do you agree that you have got memories of your honeymoon registered in your mind forever?   YES / NO
2. Do you accept that even the emperor of the world cannot buy the gone moments of life?   YES / NO

3.   Do you realize that there is a desperate need to live in the present?   YES / NO

4.   Do you think that it is crucial to watch your anger, words, actions, and responses in life?   YES / NO

5.   Do you agree that you create tantrums in the home physically, or otherwise, if your wife does not fulfill your physical demands?   YES / NO

6.   Do you think that it is imperative to thank your wife, apologies, and show gratitude at times if required? YES / NO

7.   Do you agree that you take things lightly in life and behave like a careless person?   YES / NO

8.   Have you ever asked yourself whether marrying her was the right decision or not?   YES / NO

9.   Have you ever asked your wife whether she got satisfied after the process?   YES / NO

10.   Do you agree that there is a need for a lot of refurbishment in your personality?   YES / NO

Phase Seven
The Golden Time of Nine Months

"It is the most powerful creation to have life growing inside of you. There is no bigger gift."

- Beyonce

"In pregnancy, there are two bodies, one inside the other. Two people live under one skin. When so much of life is dedicated to maintaining our integrity as distinct beings, this bodily tandem is an uncanny fact."

- Joan Raphael-Leff

Bravo!! Congratulations!

You are going to be the father. The Good News reached to you. What a lucky man you are!

It is beyond words to express the feelings of a father's heart when he gets to know the news of his first child's conceiving confirmation. A life of yours is going to be with you soon. The world's most dangerous man shows emotional insight into the near and dear on hearing the news of his child. Any man in the world bends down on his knees for the sake of his child. The first child is the weak part of the heart of the strongest man in the world. A man, to whom no one can defeat, surrenders for his child. Blood is blood. It is the specialty of blood that the moment it is in front of you, the world is in one part, and the blood is in another domain.

There is an epic story in Indian scriptures about Lord Ganesh (The Lord with an elephant head). I wish to write here in a few words: It reads: "Lord Parbati incarnated his son by mud and gave Life to him. After the incarnation process, she instructed her son to guard the palace till she is inside the palace. So does her son. Meanwhile, Lord Shiva approached and wanted to enter the palace. He was unaware that his son was guarding the palace and not letting Lord Shiva into the palace. There was a huge fight between the father and the son. As a victory, Lord Shiva cut his son's head down and entered the palace. After meeting Goddess Parbati when he came to know that he had cut his own son's head. He instructed his disciples to get the cut head of any first alive creature to him. So the disciples brought the head of an elephant. Lord Shiva placed the head on the body of his son and brought him to life. This is how the son gets the name of "Lord Ganesh" because of having the elephant's head.

In my view, the supreme God created the universe as per the scriptures and had a soft corner for his son. We are humans. It is very natural to kneel for our child.

You have another biological reason that should seek your consideration to have this intense feeling. The only effort to get the child in this world is to inject the sperms, not only one but forty to three hundred million in one action. HOW MANY?

Forty to three hundred million sperms a man ejaculates in one time to get the child conceived. The beauty is out of three hundred million; only one sperm is useful and reaches up to the egg and enters inside to turn into an embryo.

A woman lays only one egg at a time. How many? ONLY ONE. Understand that Mother Nature made the woman powerful and man lenient. She comes alone at your home after marriage, although you go along with hundreds of people. She lays only one egg to conceive, and you spray three hundred million at a time. What irony is placed by Mother Nature, which a man doesn't want to understand?

The woman has much strength in comparison to the man bestowed by Mother Nature.

It is the right moment to enjoy and understand the Golden time of Nine Months of pregnancy. I wish you could do one small exercise with yourself. It is the most vital situation for you to understand the pregnancy period of your wife.

Next Sunday, take a long piece of cloth. Get at least two kilograms of sand. Pour in the sand in the fabric, seal it, and tie the material on your belly in a position that sand should be in front. Tie it tight for nine hours on your stomach. Do all routine work on the day. You must eat, drink, sleep, go to the toilet, go to the rooftop, have a walk, sit on the couch, and do all routine work. What will happen then? Nothing will happen.

This one-time nine-hour experience will give you more respect and care for your wife, who is carrying your child, your heir, inside her belly for nine long months. In pregnancy, each day is like nine months. There are three trimesters-thirty-six to forty weeks of pregnancy.

By doing this experiment, you will better understand her suffering to carry a child inside the belly? You will start caring for her in a better way. Note down your nine hours of experience for your future memory. In the future, till your last breath, whenever you feel that you wish to get separated or there are problems in your married life. Before taking a final step, you must do this nine-hour exercise by holding two kilograms of sand on your belly and making a final decision at the end of the activity. At least for sure, you will make the right decision, whatever it may be.

The golden time of nine months of the first baby from man's eyes has two ways to move forward. The beauty is that these two ways could be traveled individually or parallel. I am explaining both the practices of the thought process for you. The way you will think during this golden time of your life depends on your individual decision.

The first approach could be that you are at the top of the world. God is going to bestow you the child of yours. You will now become a father. Your world around you will get change. Your priorities will change. You will not think of yourself; instead, your focus will be on your child. You may become more responsible, more caring, and more optimistic. The first child in the Life of man could be a turning point. You will love your wife with deeper intensity. You may forget the world, and your child and wife will become your whole world. You may start saving money. You may stop drinking, and you may stop smoking. You may stop looking for chocolates as if you have achieved a state of maturity.

The news of the first child could be a natural phenomenon in a man's life to become mature in a moment. Act as a responsible father. To have the feeling that now I have to live for my child. I decided to bring the child into this world. The child did not approach me and asked me to bear to the world. I got a child. It is my responsibility. You have a great feeling, the love of yours, with your first creation in your heart. I am in love with my book while writing as it is the first-ever creation of my life. You feel the love with your first-ever painting, first business, first job, and above all, with your first love. You never forget.

So there are chances that you will also take a rebirth along with your child.

The second approach; you will be happy about receiving the news of your first child's birth. One day you will visit the doctor along with your wife. The doctor advises you that you must not have intimate relations with your wife for the next twelve to fifteen months. (Suppose you visit a doctor during the initial month). The Everest has fallen. Gosh!! I can't have fifteen months of sleep without the release of my energy. You may ask for an alternative solution from the doctor separately. To the dismay of yours, the doctor, by frowning eyebrows, informs you that it could be fatal for your child and wife both.

Doctor says, KEEP OFF!

You are helpless. You may probably instruct your hands to take charge of your wife for the next twelve to fifteen months. Hands being a slave of yours bonded to follow your instructions, fulfill their duty like a dutiful genie of "Aladdin's lamp."

It is a very crucial point of your Life. It could also be a turning point in your life. You could become an utterly irresponsible man for your family. You have only one goal in Life to satiate your physical impulse by hook or by crook. If your pocket allows, you may start releasing all your energies through your pocket. The problem here is that the pocket does not satiate your emotional and physical impulse. You get your energy released the way you want, but without the emotional bonding. You can better understand that you may get a rubber doll to play with some soft, smooth touch and feel of skin. The notable point is that without any response of breathing ups & down. Without various sounds, take you to the top of Everest, warmth, bearing of pain, suffering, your dominance, still showing enjoyment and fun. Fulfillment of your unscrupulous demands with a response of more from the wife, and the height of Everest grows. Gosh!! She prays to God at that time; God makes him release fast, mercy me. You keep on continuing with the products available in the market to grow the Everest of yours as if you will never be able to grow without that world. What is the point?

The point is that your brain will shift its place below the belly during your wife's pregnancy. The doctor says you must not eat chocolate at home due to the health risk. You start a search for the chocolate outside and make sure that no one could get the information about it. You may or may not be successful. I am concerned about your wife. The way she took pains for you till now and these nine months will be a hell of an experience for her. Instead of understanding her situation, you are placing your brain below the belly and start neglecting her. You must have to think a hundred times, man. Why a hundred times, infinite times. After a hundred, if you count one hundred and one, your wife may start searching for me who suggested thinking for a hundred times, and her life is spoiled.

You got the point in detail that the first child's pregnancy is the crucial moment for a man to struggle not to let the brain be displaced and love his wife. You have already held fire for many years before marriage. It is hardly fifteen months. You get involved in the golden time and won't even remember that Everest exists.
Now, I will take you to your wife's journey of nine months of experience for your better understanding.

Do you have any idea of her pain in which a woman suffers at the time of delivery? You can say yes, I do have. I must say you don't have any idea. The man cannot bear the pain his wife is going to take. Man will die on the spot if he has to maintain the same endeavor.

Do you have any idea of the most dangerous fear in the heart of the girl, spinster, or a married woman? The fear is, "Oh God! How would I bear the pain of delivery?" It is her greatest fear. This feeling's psychological understanding is in fair use by commercialization and converted most of today's world deliveries as cesarean deliveries, from a tiny passage of hardly four inches a whole body of six to eight pounds passing through. Can you imagine, man? You cannot bear it. I pay gratitude to all mothers of the world to take the pain of delivery. A man will prefer to hang himself instead of experiencing the process of delivering a baby. Your wife needs your emotional support, care, and love to bear the sufferings of her pregnancy.

There are various complications she has to go through. I am taking you on the journey of multiple complications so that you can understand her sufferings and know that you must respect and "Love Your Wife." These are general issues that I am putting here for the sake of a man's understanding. So that man must think of an infinite time before leaving his wife or looking for another option. I am an observer, not a doctor.

Your wife may have Iron Deficiency Anemia; having this, she may feel tired or weak, look pale, feel faint or experience shortness of breath. Gestational Diabetes may increase the risk of a baby that is too large (macrosomia). She may fall into depression and anxiety. There are other mental health conditions during pregnancy, and after the baby is born. It can significantly impact the health of the mother and her child. Fetal problems could include decreased movement after 28 weeks of pregnancy and could lead to early delivery. Your wife could have high blood pressure; if any man could not follow the doctor's instructions and inject infections into his wife. The latter could lead to complications for his wife and the baby after delivery. Hyperemesis Gravidarum (HG) (Pronounced HEYE-pur-EM-uh-suhss grav-uh-DAR-uhm). Your wife may experience severe, persistent nausea and vomiting during pregnancy beyond the typical "morning sickness." Your wife may have Preeclampsia. It is a quick or sudden onset of high blood pressure after the twentieth week of pregnancy. She may have swelling of the hands and face, abdominal pain, blurred vision, dizziness, and headaches. The natural term of pregnancy must be for thirty-nine to forty weeks (full-term). Your child's lungs, liver, and brain go through a crucial period of growth between thirty-seven to thirty-nine weeks of pregnancy. Due to any complications or your Everest desire, if your wife has to face the preterm delivery before thirty-seven weeks, then it is perilous. There is a significant risk for your child and your wife's complications. If at all, you are the loving father of your baby and a lover of your wife, then pray to God that your baby must not face the world before thirty-nine weeks of pregnancy. Make sure that you must not contribute to bringing the baby out of the world before thirty-nine weeks by standing on the top of Everest.

(Ladies, I understand there are many complications in comparison to what I wrote here. I will take you on that journey and provide you with the solutions in detail to come out or bear the suffering with ease for you in my next title, **"Love Your Husband."**)

I assume that I took you to the journey of complications of your wife during pregnancy so that you can develop respect in your heart for your wife, and you must "Love Your Wife."

I take you on the journey of the development of your child in the mother's womb for nine months to make you understand how life grows inside, how you grew in your mother's womb.

You may ask what the use of this information is. The internet is full of the same. True, it is available out there. It matters a lot that you didn't read it. Here you are reading. I must take you through the journey to understand the emotional bonding of a mother and a child. You will have the matured thinking developed inside you by keeping the brain where God decided as the crown on your head.

Not like a protruding hanging object having no work other than having sit-ups many times a day.

The Golden nine months are divided into three trimesters by doctors, first, second, and third. In the first trimester, your baby will change from a small grouping of cells to a fetus starting to have a baby's features. By the end of the first month, your baby is about one-fourth of an inch long - smaller than a grain of rice. In the second month, your baby's facial features continue to develop. The neural tube (brain, spinal cord, and other neural tissue of the central nervous system) is well-formed now. At about six weeks, the doctor can detect your baby's heartbeat. By the end of the second month, your baby is called a fetus instead of an embryo. Now your baby is about 1 inch long and weighs about one upon thirtieth of an ounce. By the third month, your Baby's arms, hands, fingers, feet, and toes can develop in full. By the end of the third month, your baby gets its shape in full. The baby's circulatory and urinary systems are also working, and the liver produces bile. At the end of the third month, your baby is about four inches long and weighs about one ounce. By this month risk of miscarriage drops considerably.

The second trimester is the best part of the pregnancy. By this time, any morning sickness is probably gone. You may feel movement as your baby flips and turns in the uterus. In the fourth month, your baby's heartbeat may now be audible through an instrument called Doppler. Your baby can even suck his or her thumb, yawn, stretch, and make faces. By the end of the fourth month, your baby is about six inches long and weighs about four ounces. In the fifth month, the movements of the baby are exact. The first movement is called quickening and can feel like a flutter. Hair begins to grow on the head. By the end of the fifth month, your baby is about ten inches long and weighs from half to one pound. In the sixth month, if you could look inside the uterus at your baby right now, you would see that your baby's skin is reddish, wrinkled and veins are visible through the baby's translucent skin. The eyelids begin to part, and the eyes open. By the end of the sixth month, your baby is about twelve inches long and weighs about two pounds. In the seventh-month, Baby's hearing is fully developed. The baby responds to stimuli, including sound, pain, and light. At the end of the seventh month, your baby is about fourteen inches long and weighs from two to four pounds.

The third trimester is the final part of your Golden time. You may start to countdown for the last day. Throughout the third trimester, your baby will gain weight quickly. Common popular culture only mentions nine months of pregnancy, but a typical, full-term pregnancy is forty weeks. In the eighth month, you may notice that your wife feels that the baby is kicking more. The baby's brain is developing rapidly at this time. (This is the right time to talk to your baby as a father and create a connection.) Your baby can see and hear. (Make your voice identifiable to your baby by speaking to the baby.) Lungs are still immature. By the end of this month, your baby is eighteen inches long and weighs as much as five pounds. In the ninth month, the lungs are close to being fully developed. Your Baby can coordinate the reflexes so he or she can blink, close eyes, turn the head, grasp firmly, and respond to sounds, light, and touch. Your baby is about seventeen to nineteen inches long and weighs five and a half to six and a half-pound.

In the tenth month between the week thirty-seven to forty, your wife could have labor pain at any time. The moves of the baby are less due to the tight space. The position of the baby may have changed to prepare for birth. Ideally, the baby is head down in the uterus. Your wife will feel very uncomfortable in this final period as the baby drops down into her pelvis and prepares for birth. Your baby is about eighteen to twentieth inches long and weighs about seven pounds.

YOUR BABY IS READY TO MEET THE WORLD AT THIS POINT.

The final day is in your vicinity, any time your wife may have labor pain. Get ready to experience and cherish the best moments of your life. Live in the present. Forget about the past or future, any difference of opinion with any human in your life. Wait for the moment as if God is landing to deliver the baby in your hand. These moments once are gone, you can't rebuy them. Bring all your focus with full attention to feel the first being of your child in your hands. Release all stresses. Your worrying will not make any difference. Have faith in God. He has plans better than us for us. He is sending a new life on earth. You and your wife are just the transporters of life on this planet. It is God's system of lending a life on earth. You have no control over anything, not even the doctors or any other human. It is all set by God. You relax. Wait and capture the feeling in your mind on the first arrival of your baby. I feel that you are also ready to meet with your baby. You are prepared to respect and **"Love Your Wife."**

Phase Eight
Birth of Your First Child

"The moment a child is born, the mother is also born. She never existed before. The woman existed, but the mother, never. A mother is something absolutely new. And so in you, the child, your mother lives on and through your family continues to live… so at this time look after yourself and your family as you would your mother for through you all she will truly never die."

- Osho

You are moving towards the labor room as your wife has got labor pain. It could be any time out of twenty-four hours of the day. Your heart is beating as if it wants to race with you and wishes to defeat you by pooping out and jumping to cross the finish line. You cannot see your wife yelling in pain. The suffering is horrible, and you are holding her hand, trying to say, "Don't worry, everything will be alright." You are right at your place. But could you imagine her suffering? YOU CANNOT.

Till you experience it yourself, you cannot. It is impossible for me even to explain a woman's suffering after having such a keen observation of life. All the known sufferings of the world as a man, which I know are less to compare. The pain of delivery that a woman undergoes is incomparable in this world to any man or woman.

You may count as a male that, why am I mentioning in such an

93

elaborative way. This process should be like that. Every woman passes through this process. My wife is not out of Seven Wonders of the World, who is suffering.

A man is always right. I am not countering you. I am narrating the facts for the suffering of your wife, which she is bearing for you. You will get your heir. What is your contribution to bring a life into the world biologically? You spur 300 million sperm once in a lifetime for this child. God chooses you to do this. Rest all God trusted on a woman. God knows your qualities. You are a restless, impatient, egoistic man who always thinks I am the creator. A man still wants to rule the world. Every man wants that world to follow his word. If I tell anyone to sit, he/she must sit. I am the father. You cannot control your hunger, words, anger, ego, impulse, lust, emotions, and you say I want to rule. What is your role in becoming a father? You cannot bear this pain. Believe me!

YOU CANNOT.

I am running short of words and facts in life to reach the exact depiction of labor pain. Every known pain to me as a male, either physical or emotional, is less painful than a woman's pain at the time of delivery. It is impossible to bear the pain for a man. We cannot reach close to the suffering of that moment in life.

Do you have any idea why the delivery room in the hospitals is called the labor room? 'Mahatrai Ra' mentioned in one of his spiritual videos, "The extreme suffering with labor brings out a new life to the world." It is the transmutation of a female. A woman becomes a mother. Osho mentioned it in his words, which I refer to at the beginning of the chapter. Not only will the child get birth, but the mother will also take birth. In my opinion, the father will also take birth. It is a transmutation for both. A mother cannot become a woman ever. It is a transmutation as a caterpillar becomes the butterfly; now, it is impossible if the butterfly wants to be the caterpillar.

You have understood the woman's state and her strength to bear the suffering at the delivery time. It would be best if you remembered the suffering of your wife forever in the future. If you feel that you want to get separated, you cannot survive in the marriage. You must recall your wife's suffering and think if she should have survived at the time of your child's birth, then you must stay in your marriage and don't ever give up. One of the significant reasons for getting separated or having extramarital relations in marriage is a man's habit of giving up-the man gives-up (exceptions are considered). The women never give up. God's training to give birth to a baby is the best training for the woman, and she never gives-up. When we say it is a do or die situation, a life, and death situation. A woman always does or chooses life but never gives up. Man gives up in no time. If you disagree that you have a habit of giving up quickly, you write me an email. (I am not addressing the spiritual achievers; I am addressing the common man in society.) I will answer you individually to make you understand.

I will take you now through the process of delivery for a better three-sixty degree understanding. You will understand how your wife suffers for you, to whom you generally give up very quickly.
Your child's delivery process involves three stages of labor: the shortening and opening of the cervix, descent and birth of the baby, and the delivery of the placenta. The first stage typically lasts twelve to nineteen hours, the second stage twenty minutes to two hours, and the third stage for five to thirty minutes.

You may question; the use of this information to a common man who does not belong to the medical field?

I tell you what the use is for a common man.

A common man is generally not allowed inside the labor room. In some of the developed countries, it may be the latest practice. They allow the father to be with the mother at the time of delivery for her emotional support. Very few men get this chance. In general, it is not in everyday practice.

The reverse is also possible that a common man does not choose to be inside the labor room based on various reasons.

In general, a man is not at all aware of what happened in the labor room. He knows that there is a severe pain to my wife, which she will bear somehow and deliver the child. My friend, God, has not created a simple process to produce a new life on this earth. The woman inside will have an experience of hell. I wish you must know at least if you cannot experience it yourself. My objective is that; you must have deep respect and intense love for your wife that she is suffering because of you. You often mention that you cannot see your wife in suffering, the pain of hers, blood inside the labor room. It is all mere excuses of you, to whom you tell a lie, to yourself or the world. You are the reason for sending her to get an heir of your property. You want a baby who will carry your name forward in the world. You want someone to be there to produce the next generation of your family. At the same time, you are saying I cannot see her in pain. What humor you are creating, and the world agrees with you. You keep on hiding the facts, tell a lie, and everyone keeps on believing. The suffering woman is lying inside the labor room on the table, keeping her both legs open up in the sky and going through the pain of hell.

Stop freaking out. Accept the fact that you are the reason for suffering. I agree this is the process; every woman has to go through to deliver a baby. I am not telling you to stop producing children. My point is to the husband that you must respect and love your wife and stand with her inside and watch your child coming out in blood. Then you will never leave her in life. You like the heart's red color on every New Year, Valentine's Day, or on your anniversary, and you bring red roses, a red heart, and red gifts. That means you like RED. Then why are you reluctant to see the blood? See it, feel it, and cherish it in your heart for your wife for how much blood she sheds to give birth to your baby. If you think of leaving her or look for another option, think of the labor room and then decide.

Do you have any idea why your wife has pain before labor? As I have mentioned above, there are three stages of labor. The first stage begins with uterine contractions and ends with complete cervical dilatation at ten cm. The contractions are like sea waves, severe strong waves approaching the shore, and hit with tragic pressure at various intervals. The same is the feeling inside your wife. It is the reason she yells in breaks. These contractions last from twelve to nineteen hours or less. You imagine your wife bearing this pain, and you are ready to leave. God must help you. I have seen my wife yelling for twelve hours in this pain, and I have experienced that pain in me. My heart was throbbing at double speed, and the doctor was trying for standard delivery. Wife yelling out of pain, the doctor yelling, "Push," take a deep breath, "Push." You cannot bear all this as a man.

The second stage starts with cervical dilatation and ends with the delivery of the fetus. An ideal situation if your baby is head down and in a position to come out, then in the second stage, the head of the baby comes out first. It is called crowning. Sometimes, suppose the head doesn't come out. In that case, doctors use external devices such as a mild vacuum pump called vacuum extractions or vacuum-assisted delivery. Once the crown is out, the doctor pulls the shoulder, limb, and whole body of your baby. It is attached to an umbilical cord with the placenta. The umbilical cord is the arrangement to provide all sorts of nourishment to your baby inside the mother's womb. It has to cut. It is the first-ever experience of sheer pain to your baby when he/she enters the world. Remember, all the nerves pass through the umbilical cord via the belly button of the human body. The doctor cut it. The pain gets registered in the brain and body cells of the baby. It is the reason being an adult when you take a high swing or do an adventure activity, and you feel a deep fear wave near your belly button. Since birth at the belly button, your body has the fear and pain registered, so it recalls always.

Once your baby is out, the doctor cuts the umbilical cord and then starts the third stage. The delivery of the placenta and fetal membrane takes place. The placenta is an organ that develops during pregnancy to provide oxygen and nutrients to your baby. It also removes waste products from your baby's blood. The umbilical cord arises from it. Once the baby is delivered, the placenta has no use in your wife's body. So it also gets delivered and brings out all amniotic fluid and blood, which holds your baby for nine months.

Every man must experience this process and should develop a deep respect and intense love for his wife. **You must "Love Your Wife" for delivering your baby. It is the reason you must say "I Love You" and thank you to your wife every day till your or her last breath.**

The doctor brings out your baby from the labor room-heartiest congratulations to the mother and father. You have got your baby in your hand.

I feel my first daughter, "Joell," in my hands when writing this paragraph for you. It is so lively that I am standing right now, and the doctor brought her out and gave her in my hands. It is excellent, unbelievable, and the feelings live in my mind that a scientist could have designed a machine that can convert brain memories into a live video. You will have an awesome momentary video to cherish. Along with the daughter, a father took birth. I took rebirth at that time.

Thank you, God, for bestowing me the fatherhood.

Phase Nine
First Five Years of Your Child

"True wisdom comes to each of us when we realize how little we understand about life, ourselves, and the world around us."

- Socrates

You are happy to become a father. Fatherhood is the best gift of God. You are reborn, along with your child, and enjoy the selfless love, hope, aspirations, and care in the eyes of your child. At the same time, you shower all your love, care, and wealth on to your child. You will earn and fulfill all demands of your child in the future. You hope that your child should give you an opportunity that people recognize you as the proud father of a successful human in future years. You wish that whatever you earn in this materialistic world, your child must take it to the next level. You want your child to carve his/her name on the stone. You wish that whatever fields your child will choose as a career, he must reach on top. Suppose dance is the field, then your child should be Michel Jackson. If Cricket is the field, then your child must be Virat Kohli. If music is the field of work, and then your child must be among the Beatles. If science is the field of work, then your child must be Albert Einstein. Medicine is the field then, Dr. Naresh Trehan. Assume engineering is the field of work of the Wright brothers. You have your list of expectations set in the subconscious mind and sometimes in the conscious mind too.

The world will look for the resemblance of your features in your child. They will compare the nose, eyes, skin tone, voice, physic, and many more aspects of both father and the child. You will feel elevated, happy, and proud of this comparison. Your ego is at the top, having this comparison of your features with your child. Your child may have the speaking tone, walking style, eating style, seating style, writing style, and many more resemblances of your personality. Whenever you receive your child's praised comparison with you, it will give you a proud feeling. You may have a proud sense of spurring such a potent sperm to get almost a clone of yourself. If you need to select between your wife and your child, your inclination would be to your sperm. You keep your child above your wife. Deep in your heart, you feel 'my child' because of my sperm. You quickly forget the pain and suffering of your wife. Don't forget! Your wife showed the way to your sperm to the world.

It is essential to remember your wife's pain and suffering and always keep her place above everything in your life. Whenever we keep someone above all, we never leave that person in any troublesome situation in life. A father never leaves his child; in suffering.

Why does the husband do so?

The same human acts differently as a father and a husband. It is because of your attitude towards fatherhood and being a husband. Everything which is your natural part you love a lot. Your wife is also your natural part; **THINK**, isn't she? Your wife takes you in her body, and this is how she is also your biology. It would be best to change your attitude towards her, and you will never leave your wife. Everyone else except your wife, who takes you in, has a purpose of fulfilling. It is only your wife who takes you in with love and without a purpose. A lover has the goal of winning you as a husband. A wife has no intent to achieve. Think in a deep sense and apply all your experiences. You will find the above statement accurate on account of being a male. (This could be discussed individually for any particular case; via email communication if you wish to; write me one.)

Compare the world's attitude between the wife and the child. The world of comedy is full of humor for husband and wife. There are jokes; you enjoy for your wife. Everyone who wants these touches of humor gets the secretion of serotonin in the brain. I have never come across a joke on the father and his son or daughter in a sarcastic way. The feeling of mine is attached to the relationship between father and children. The same is missing in the relationship between husband and wife. Man treats his wife for the fulfillment of two basic desires of his life. One is to satiate the physical starvation. The second is to get the heir for his property, name, and legacy to carry forward after his death.

The obnoxious reality is that no man has any device or solution available to confirm that the name, fame, and wealth created by him is in an advanced stage or diminished after his death. The child on whom every man is proud can take it to the next level or, in reality, bring it down. The wealth acquired for seven generations, is it sufficient for this one generation or not. History is full of examples. I won't mention the name of anyone. No emperors and empires are existing who have acquired wealth and property. Heirs in history took the wealth to the next level, but where is the creator of wealth to check and be happy that wow! My son did whatever I thought. You will not be present in the world to check whether your name is in an advanced stage or diminished.

Why is everyone running behind the fatherhood, leaving the husband behind? Care for your wife, and "Love your wife."

103

Your wife and your child are at home. You are a proud father for the world, and you will keep on showing happiness to the world. Everyone praises you and congratulates you on the successful result of your sperm. Within a week or months, the other side of the coin will be visible. I am taking you through the journey of your child's upbringing for the first five years from birth. I am putting efforts to show your behavior and thinking patterns during these five years towards your wife. Every father loves the child. The child is not the center to talk. Most husbands make their wives responsible for every problem that comes on their way during the child's upbringing. The picture is not rosy; the days are not always happy. Within a week or a month, the first inner voice of man asks himself. When will she heal or be ready for intimate relations?

It is almost nine to ten months. The hungry horse is getting mad. The doctor says to wait, and you cannot. Your wife comes up with a solution to balance the situation. Every wife knows to handle the situation. She is ready to bear some more pain, which will be less compared to the recent one. She will understand you, and what about you. Do you know her physical situation? Whatever I have explained in the previous phase about your baby's delivery, there is more than that. It might be possible that your wife may go through the episiotomy, also known as perineotomy. The healing of which is a long process and your wife has to bear the pain for many days. In this situation, your demand for the fulfillment of physical needs is the most despotic. The beauty is that she is ready to fulfill out of your love. You must love your wife for this sweetness. How sweet she is for you, and you leave her or are prepared to take a divorce, mentioning that she does not belong to your type.

Think about it.

The whole family is in routine, except one, the mother of the child.

The child will present a new challenge every day. A working woman has to face more difficulties in life as she manages the child, the home, the husband, and the job. Everyone in her life will cry, the child will cry, you the husband will cry for cravings, the boss will call for the deadline, and others I cannot mention. The woman will wipe off everyone's tears by not letting her tears find a way to roll down her eyes.

You may have a very hectic and stressful day in the office. You reach home, want to sleep, and your child is crying. You are not able to sleep. You make your wife responsible for the same. She is not able to handle the child. Do you have any idea what suffering she went through the whole day? Your wife may have a stressful day in her office. The child might have got some severe symptoms of an illness. There are various challenges which no one can pen down in a book. The importance is that you must understand her situation before getting angry or making her responsible for every problem of your life.

Your wife has priorities in life, which are all primary. There are no secondary priorities in her life. She has to be attentive to the child, in the kitchen, at the office, and on the bed. It might be possible that the child is feeding on one side and you on the other side, and she is showering her love on both suffering out of pain or stress due to any reason. A woman is the strongest on the earth that can bear emotional and physical problems altogether and show love simultaneously. That is why God chooses her to be the mother, and you are the sprayer of sperms and nothing else.

I am taking you through a brief journey of five years of the upbringing of your child. I will discuss in detail and depth the parenting and developments of your child in my third title of this series, *"Love Your Children."*

The first five years of your child's development shows a rapid change in the child. Physical growth, brain development, and cognitive development occur fast in the child's life journey. Who is the supreme caretaker of your child? Your loving wife is the caretaker.

Do you have any idea that at how many fronts your wife involves herself in a daily battle? She remains attentive to her child. During the golden time of the nine months, the biological cycle of your child has no fixed pattern. Generally, the infants sleep in the daytime and remain awake at night. What does an infant do at night? Either he feeds on his mother or cries. Whatever your child is doing, your wife has to remain awake. A mother gets a rare chance to sleep for the first six months after the child's delivery, till the child gets settled in the normal biological cycle.

The first six months of a child's upbringing have the following challenges which your wife faces:

- The child does not know the language other than crying.
- The child does not have toilet training other than crying.
- The child does not understand anything other than his mother's touch and so always cries in need.
- All family members play with the child till he/she is not crying. Your child starts crying; everyone, including you, handover him/her to the mother.
- The child knows only one human in the world, the mother.

Till the age of five years, a child learns everything by imitating. The child will learn to crawl, walk, speak his mother tongue, play, read, write, and all the necessary skills until five years. The brain is in the developmental process up to the age of five years. Who teaches everything to the child? The obvious answer is the mother first and then the family and the surrounding atmosphere. Do you teach anything to your child?

In my opinion, no father teaches anything to the child directly up to the age of five years. But he teaches indirectly. All the family members, including you, need your wife for different purposes. It would be best if you had your wife for your daily needs. Your wife needs to take care of your food. Your old age parents and their requirements also need attention. Your wife will satiate your baby's hunger by feeding and of all family members by managing food. She will satisfy you in bed. She will keep the house neat and tidy. Suppose your wife is a working woman either in service or in business, so she has to take care of those ventures too. Everyone on all fronts expects the woman to be the winner.

Your child wants the mother to feed immediately after crying. You want your food on time, your clothes washed and ironed on time. Your house must remain tidy at all times. Your parents want their tea, food, medicines on time without the delay of a single minute. The customers, bosses, and colleagues expect to meet all the required deadlines of her workplace. She does meet the expectations of everyone in her close vicinity. You, the husband, say that "She is Not Good." (You must THINK many times before narrating the statement.)

Do you have any idea of her emotional state? How much strength does she need to hold the pressure due to all the above situations in her life? The pressure is not for one day, but a lifetime a mother bears irrespective of society's religion and level; she belongs to this world.

Believe me; you have no idea of all this. A male's upbringing in the world is not to understand the emotional state of a female. I firmly

Love Your Wife

believe that if the male will get psychological training to understand females' situation from infancy. The crime rate for rape and physical assault against women will go in minus within twenty-five years in the whole world.

Who is responsible for giving the training?

A mother is responsible for the course. But you, who dominate society, play a more significant important role than her. You can raise your son with the feeling of treating not only his sister but other younger or older female folks around him with great respect. I firmly believe that the mother does not develop her daughter's environment to be treated respectfully since childhood. Every criminal of the world is not an alien. He took birth from the womb of a female. He was not a criminal when he was born. The lack of training on emotional self to the child, and no stopping during childhood when he committed the first-ever offense in his life, encouraged him to do the same for years. In the future, a day occurs in a child's life that he commits a heinous crime. All the dangerous criminals, if they are balanced psychologically, love their mother. It means they have emotions.

I am not going out of track. I will explain in detail about giving this personal training to children in my third title of this series, **"Love Your Children."** In continuation, the other title will be **"Love Your Parents."** I mentioned here the theme of the current phase of life.

My point of reference for you is; that, the female who takes such pressure for you on herself, you are ready to leave her. There are trivial issues in a couple's life on which they feel suffocated. The top reason for suffocation for a male is:

"She does not do what I Say............"

She does not sleep when I say.

She does not cook what I say.

She does not wear the dress, which I say.

She does not visit the bed when I say.

She does not get ready when I say.

She does not keep the baby well, as I say.

She does not carry herself the way I say.

Numerous points as per the religion, clan, and class of living are available with every man in the world.

My question to you is: Why would she do whatever you say?

Is she a slave of yours?

Think.

I have mentioned earlier that the institution called marriage is an arrangement or contract for two people to satiate their desires, which others cannot do. Man in the world has started taking this simple contract as a slavery contract.

Man wants to rule a woman. Emotionally and psychologically, a man is weaker than a woman.

That is why men show physical supremacy over the woman and want to rule because physically, man is supreme. Whenever any woman opposes this power and rule, a man feels suffocated. Man has a habit of giving up. Man gives-up in marriage also. You want another option and think that your life will settle down.

Love Your Wife

NO, Never.

The problem area does not lie in your wife; it lies in you.
Whatever number of marriages you do in life, you will never get settled.

You have to bring changes in you to live a joyous married life.

Phase Ten

TEN Years of Your Married Life

"He who is not contented with what he has would not be contented with what he would like to have."

- Socrate

You have crossed five years of your child's upbringing. The child has started attending school. It might be possible that during these five years, you have become a proud father of one more child. The same processes of everything your wife had gone through at the time of the second baby too. You and your wife will have a routine and monotonous life. By the sixth and seventh year of your married life, your single or both children are going to school. You are settled in your job, by promotion or by switching your company and attaining growth in your life.

The routine in your life is gel-like sugar in the water. A typical pattern where you will get up in the morning as per your schedule. Follow your morning routine of sleeping, warm-up or meditation or social media, etc. Order tea or coffee or energy drink of Aloe Vera, gourd, etc., as per your choice to your wife. Get ready or take your morning dose of chocolate as per the family situation. You will order breakfast ; to your wife, eat it, and leave for the office. You will reach back home in the evening or at night, after having a hectic or comfortable day along with the stress of your work. You bring your office home. You may not or may take the energy

111

generated in the office due to stress at home and release it on your family members.

I understand well that a man suffers various stresses during work. I am putting some of the reasons for anxiety for a common man here for reference:

You may have project completion stress. Sales target achievement stress, a lousy boss to handle, not getting time to take your lunch, not getting a raise after putting sweat and blood into the company and feeling stressed, a colleague who has got a promotion by flattery, and you are under stress, salary is not sufficient, and the EMI payment is due, creating pressure on you. Kids or parents are demanding something which you are not able to fulfill and having stress.

Your salary gets disbursed on the fifth day of the month. On the seventh day, your bank account reaches the minimum balance or overdue your credit card, creating stress.

You reach home daily by having one or the other kind of stresses in your mind. I cannot list all sorts of tensions. Stress reasons dependent on the profile of the person. A Billionaire may have a kind of stress that no one in the world could ever have. I am pointing to a state of mind, STRESS.

Every man needs stress busters. Type of stress busters could be different, like meditation, yoga, evening walk, having an evening chocolate dose, drinking alcohol, smoking, tobacco, etc. All these are external stress busters; this is how you feel. **None of the above stress busters works if you are not peaceful from your inner world.** No man requires any stress buster if he is calm from inside and learns to live in the present. Most men are turbulent in their inner world. When there is turbulence inside you, you want to vomit mentally or physically. You better do it well, else you will be disturbed. Under stressful conditions, you find faults in every work at home: The food will be tasteless, prepared by your wife. Your kids will behave manner less with you. You see an untidy house. Your wife is talking to her mom, sister, or friend when you reach home and feel suffocated on various other points.

Various trigger points tempt you to vomit mentally, and you get triggered. You start raising your voice and get angry with your wife. Some may physically assault their wife or kids. Some may begin taking alcohol too much. It may seem that the outside world has the switch; of your life in its hands. Someone else switches on, and you start acting.

For a joyous married life, the switch must be in your control. It means you should have patience, calmness, coolness, and mature behavior in your personality. The sixth-year to the tenth year of your married life are critical years for two reasons. First is that your children are watching you closely. Your children watch your behavior, habits, words, language, and routine with focused attention. You must be ready to experience the same thing with your kids once they reach teenage and adulthood. Second is, your wife will reach a stage of making a negative opinion about you as a person. Before this stage, she has not thought so. For her, you are a sweet loving husband. Your wife has suffered all the pains of delivery of your children and maintaining the family. She has learned your family's traditions and performed all the rituals as per your family's likes and dislikes. She knows all the relatives and friends of yours. She maintains a good relationship with all your acquaintances. She was managing everything as per your preferences and sacrificed all her wishes till now. Your wife knows by this stage that she has done enough for you and the family.

What is your stand for your wife's sacrifices? Do you value all her sacrifices or NOT?

She analyses the answers by observing your behavior in general. If you show her love and compassion, she feels happy and keeps on doing everything beyond her limits for you and the family. Opposite to it, suppose you show a control freak's behavior, ignore her, behave as if you want her only in the night, then she understands it well. In today's world, women are empowered. They are not ready to tolerate a control freak guy, or they can't become the slave of yours. You respect, value her sacrifices in your life, and love her from the depth of your heart honestly.

Have you ever thought of it?

- Why is there a sudden rise in the divorce rate worldwide?
- Why is there an inclination towards gay or lesbian relationships openly?
- How is the term LGBT coined in the recent history of twenty years openly?
- You can trace the institution called marriage in history for thousands of years. Couples were living in harmony. They were living their full life with the same spouse. **Agree!!**

Let's think from a different perspective:-

Humankind invented the institution called marriage thousands of years ago. The initial population of the earth was limited. Today's population of the planet is more than seven Billion. What is the origin of these many people? Are some of us aliens?

NO

We all took birth from our mother's womb. I understand that a minuscule percentage of us belong to parents who have not married; it's okay. The major belongs to the married parents. The marriages which were working for thousands of years have suddenly stopped working.

WHY?

In phase one of life, I have mentioned that the invention of marriage had the purpose of family, heir, and an individual's legacy. Who wants an inheritance and an heir?

YOU

The man wants an heir and a name or a clan producer to carry forward his name.

Have you ever heard a woman want her name on the next level in the world through her children? This world knows every successful personality by the father's name primarily.

Who is egoistic?

YOU

To satisfy his ego, the man had never empowered the woman in history. The woman did not receive a formal education. The place of the woman was always secondary. The woman got suppression in society for ages. Man ruled the world and is still leading.
Are you convinced?

YES....... NO......... MAYBE

Suppose you are not convinced. I can put some more facts as food for your mind.

Have you ever heard of an ancient time, an escort service for men to satisfy women's physical desires in the market? (I am purposely neglecting the name Gigolo from the recent past). The man was marrying too many women. There are no records of any woman having more than one husband in a house and living legally in humanity's developmental phase. (I am purposefully not quoting "Mahabharata" due to the uniqueness of its kind.) The man was visiting the market to satisfy his physical desire. The woman was content at home with her husband. Today also, the woman is content at home. It is all about a man who has issues everywhere in his married life.

The **irony** is; irrespective of a man's ability to satisfy his wife, she is happy and content. Doing everything and taking all the pain for her husband, the man is not satisfied at home with his wife. Even outside the house, he is not happy. The man keeps on changing his destination. Why do you want an escort service, if the satisfaction is available at home? I hope you are satisfied that a man has not let a woman be powerful.

What happened now?

Since globalization, the woman is educated and empowered now. Women understood well that man is using her, and she is not ready to be ruled by a man like a slave. She has understood her independent identity. The woman has learned to control her desires and does not need a man to satiate her physical desires at the cost of slavery. She has found other options of either being into a live-in relationship or being a lesbian. She is happy with either or both, as she is her own master and keeps the control switch in her hand.

Remember, it is a man who needs a woman to satiate her physical desire. The woman does not need it. Women can live a full life without physical satisfaction; Man may have issues living without a woman whole life (leaving spiritual disciples). Man has a craving for the body many times in a day; a woman does not.

Man does not have any option. Man has to choose to be gay. No one can help it; man is responsible for this scenario. You may understand the deeply rooted meaning to know what I want to convey in the above sentence.

Another option is divorce and finding another partner. You will repeat the same thing with another woman and divorce her too. A man who is not satisfied with what he has will never be happy with what he will have.

Why?

It is because the problem is not with the other person but the man himself.

What is the solution then?

- The solution is simple:
- Understand the pains she took for you.
- Stop making her your slave.
- Value her presence in your life.
- Value her decisions in life.
- Respect your wife.
- Remain honest with your wife.
- Have compassion for her.

AND

"Love Your Wife"

Soumitra Singh Thakur

TWENTY Years of Your Married Life

"The real act of marriage takes place in the heart, not in the ballroom or church or synagogue. It's a choice you make - not just on your wedding day, but over and over again - and that choice is reflected in the way you treat your husband or wife."

- Barbara De Angelis

It's an outstanding achievement that you have crossed ten years of married life with the same spouse. The term is rare globally in the twenty-first century and on the verge of extinction in the twenty-second century. Medical research is in the advanced stage and on the point of prolonging a human's lifespan. I am sure that the humans taking birth in the thirties of the twenty-first century will look at the sunrise of 1st January 2101. In the twenty-second century, people will laugh at the institution called marriage. They won't believe how their grandparents would have lived and slept with the same spouses for thirty or forty years in life. They may doubt the term grandparents too.

Today, the present time is in our hands, and if we wish that the above scenario must not arise. We must start nurturing the institution called marriage the way it was at its inception back in history. **Marriage is delicate. You have to handle it with care.**

Ten to twenty years of your marriage is the essential phase of your life for your kids. During this phase, your kids will reach teenage and adulthood. You will grow in your life with financial stability on the heap of EMI. You will gather every materialistic support system for your family by arranging it on EMI. Your age is approaching in the forties. You think that I will work twenty-four by seven to take early retirement and enjoy life with my family. You do not give time to your family and save it for the future. You don't know how your kids are growing in their teenage years. Who are the friends of your kids? What is the status of your kids learning by observing you, from friends, and from strangers about whom you are unaware? How is the internet teaching your kids, and what?

You depend on your wife to take care of all the above aspects of your kid's life. You are busy earning for them. You are doing all the hard-work for whom? You are doing it for your kids and family. You do not require anything for yourself. You have no desire for yourself. In this manner, you claim and put excuses for not paying attention to your wife and kids. Often, kids don't know for a week or a month that their father remains present in the home. Do they have their father in life? They get astonished at times.

Your wife manages the home. If she is a working woman, she helps you financially, emotionally, and satisfies you physically. During the married life of twenty years, it might be possible that you have old age retired parents at home. Your wife needs to take care of them as if you and your parents are the responsibility of your wife and not yours. You feel that your duty is to earn money. By making money, you think that all your obligations are over. Rest everything is the responsibility of your wife. Gone are the days when this deep-rooted unaccepted thought of yours was of worth.
The woman is empowered now. She is smart, bold, self-dependent, confident, and a firm decision-maker in today's society. You are working outside; she is working inside. You are the one side of the

coin; she is the other side of the coin. A currency of one side is not of any use. Your wife is the equal part of the institution called marriage. If you wish to suppress her, she will rebel. She will put her point. She wants her presence in the decision making process for the family. You cannot make a woman fool now as she uses her intellect. The early humans have thought of these consequences of the power of woman intellect very well. That is why they made the necessary arrangements with every possible aspect to suppress the woman in humankind. They knew very well that if the woman is empowered, she will rule the world. I can foresee the situation in the future twenty-second or twenty-third century.

For survival's sake, a man needs a woman. A common man is not in a position to control his physical cravings. A man needs a woman. Opposite to it, a woman without attending any sermon and without being inclined towards spirituality can control her physical hunger for a lifetime. It's easy for her.

What is your stand in your married life?

You ignore your wife. Whatever you do, you do it for the formality to maintain a relationship. You may get a seven to nine months tummy for yourself. Your wife kept it for nine months only, and you are keeping it forever. You have your excuses and justifications for not walking, not exercising, or not doing yoga, or not able to control your taste buds and hunger. Your drinking and smoking are at their peak due to stress at work or your job. Now and then, some of you want the most beautiful woman in your bed and wish that your wife must maintain her figure. You have various complaints about her figure as if her husband is the mister universe with six-packs.

As per the global divorce rate of various countries, most marriages are not reaching this married life phase. They are starting their inning again by this age. Every man who starts a second or third inning will get nothing new except a bit of adventure to satiate his craving for physical desires. Man is a lover of adventures everywhere. Man has a deep inner thought to reveal the hidden. Learned psychologists did various psychological experiments to understand this feeling of a man to know the invisible.

There is nothing on the note of physical desires hidden between you two in the married life of ten to twenty years. So you get nothing new to unhide and want something new, irrespective of this understanding that the latest has everything the same as the old. The second inning has its beauty of freshness and nothing else. Have you noticed that a second-hand man wants to put his first step on the moon? He wants to have a fresh experience irrespective of his; that is not fresh. Don't you feel an irony here? It is a matter of obtainability that he may or may not get a chance to come across fresh experience, then he moves to the second-hand episode. That too, he wants to have thought he would get something new. He gets nothing new, and soon he wants to start the third inning. Generally, the term of the second and third innings is lesser than the first inning. I accept the exceptions.

There are ample chances that man won't go for a second or third inning. Instead, he will remain in the same relationship of first marriage. He then starts looking for options outside the home and learns to manage and enjoy both inside and outside cravings of his physical desires. You may think this is not the case with all. I do agree. Suppose you look inside yourself or any of your colleagues, friends in your known circle. You may notice that they have one or two options in their target and want to reach on a bed in due course of time. Suppose bed is not the destination with any of the opposite gender. In that case, the person's behavior and dealings will remain at the highest level of decency. You act in a thoroughly professional way that no one can raise a finger on you. Once the journey with one destination is over, you look for another port of call by making your way. It keeps on going in your life.

What do I want to prove as an author?

I set my heart to mention that whatever escapade and craving for revealing hidden you possess, you can consummate with your wife. It would be better if you focused attention on your wife. She is the most beautiful woman on earth by mind, body, and soul. You have to learn to value her. She can effectuate all your adventures with the best complacency of yours. You need to start looking for exploring this option inside instead of exploring it outside.

How?

My answer to this is that man has a basic instinct to reconnoitering if he wants it and likes it. You have to develop that want and liking in yourself for your wife. No one in the world, including counselors, psychologists, and I, can help in this exploration journey of you two. You are the right person who has to find a way out. You can do so; there is a need for preparation to be done. That's all.

Once you are ready to explore the world between you two, you will enjoy it the way you made whoopee on your copulating night. It could be as fresh as the first experience.
You can live in the present every day by loving your wife, and life will be harmonious forever.

Phase Twelve
THIRTY Years of Your Married Life

"After three decades, we know each other well. We know the quirks and the pet peeves. We know how to make each other yell. But our strength is what 30 years weaves."

- Anonymous

Pat your back!!

You have crossed twenty years of married life. It's a significant achievement. During the decade of thirties, you will celebrate the Silver Jubilee of your married life. You have a chance to recreate the marriage function. You can invite all the friends and relatives who had attended your marriage twenty-five years ago once again. Some might have departed from this planet, but many can join you back.

Have you thought of a significant difference between the marriage day and the silver jubilee? The difference is time. Time brought a substantial change in everyone. Greying hair, fat on the body, less power, lesser enthusiasm, and above all, you have turned mature.

Suppose you wish to recreate the night of copulating once again after the silver jubilee. In that case, you cannot have the same strength, stiffness, prolonged time, and fun the way you enjoyed the first time. You and your wife are in the fifties by this time. You may need lubricants and supplements to maintain your prolonged pleasures.

My point is that after twenty-five or more years of your marriage, you come to know that the manhood on which you were relying so much is not eternal. Manhood, which was the cynosure of your thoughts for twenty-five or more years, and you might have tested your strength with many partners, is deteriorating slowly. The energy available with ample amount to use even four times or more in a day for twenty plus years is not that much with you now.

The irony is that living in a marriage with the same spouse or with a second or third, the energy will not remain with you. Your position in your mind will remain the same irrespective of the partner number. The Furness has gone cold. The self-fuel is no more with you. Self-fuel of your thoughts that you think and get a standing ovation has gone. You keep on thinking, and it will take a longer time to happen. It will work with immense effort. Now you will occupy with so much effort to think and put in supplements so that you can get glimpses of the enjoyed energy. The sand which you held for many years is no more in hands.

What will you do now? You will increase the doses of supplements or may visit a doctor to seek help. Don't worry; hardly anything is going to work for anyone. It is about to go.

Are you able to accept the fact?

NO

Probability says that you won't be able to come out of your cynosure thoughts even in your nineties. You will spend time on the internet. You will have your friends group, where you will share

Soumitra Singh Thakur

your thoughts on social media personally. You may be moving towards becoming a grandfather. But still, you want to be a father again, THINK! You are aware that you cannot. You use mobile to satiate. Keep it locked in your safe custody.

Your wife is helpless on you, the poor guy. She tries a lot to get you the standing ovation. She had suffered many times in her life due to your standing ovations. She laughs and pities you inside. What is your role in this scenario? You may blame her for the situation of yours, which she never understands. How is she responsible? Doctors will give detailed guidance to you. If Mother Nature would not have created this deterioration process, then there was no need for a considerable lubricant market and supplements on the planet. Why has this industry been on a boom always since ancient times? The reason is; that; man cannot come out of his thoughts and never accepts that his energy source is cold now. He remains hovering in the same ideas. The vision of the world has changed for you. You are older, and youth is gone. You are in the category of uncle. You don't accept it. You dye your hair to disguise the world as young. You stare, and youth catches your eyes and laugh at you. You feel no one is watching. Everyone is watching you except you. Your daughter-in-law or son-in-law is in your life. You still behave as if you are in your thirties.

You attend sermons and preaching sessions. Participate in debates of maturity; you start depicting as a mature man. Sitting in front of the priest or saint and staring at the beautiful roses available in the hall. No one who gives public preaching is omniscient. You are at the best place to hover in thoughts of standing ovation with various roses available in the hall. (Only in thoughts and not in reality). No one will be able to know. The world judges you with your external appearance and your speech. Internal thoughts are yours only, and you enjoy this state. You may think that this is not true. I agree.

It is true with "Most" men in the world but not with you. You may or may not belong to the "Most" category. In the case of NO, you try to find out a percentage of people who attend the spiritual sermons, follow your age's spiritual gurus, and are enlightened.

The media and internet are full of the stories which I wish to narrate here but would not. A person on a dais, preaching, and not following found guilty shows the difference between everyone's words and thoughts. What is the reason for the difference between words and thoughts? Why do the words and actions always mismatch with "Most" of the men in the world? The reason is straightforward but not easy to accept.

Man has no self-control.

You are not able to control your desire to look younger. You cannot control your hunger, words, anger, ego, and almost everything in your life. You live in society and not in the jungle. You have to follow the rules of society and cannot live like a tribal person. You found a way out. You show; what the community wants from you. You depict yourself as a mature, decent, disciplined, religious, trustworthy, well-mannered man of words who could be the role model for youth. Inside you, you are you. You know who you are. I am not mentioning a single word to clarify who you are. If I do so, the book will go for a thousand pages. **You decide what you inside are.**

The best way for you to prove me wrong is to watch your words and actions for a week.

You praise someone for decent attire. Do you praise or abuse from your inside?

You praise someone for a lovely recipe. Do you praise or want to finish the dish somehow?

You praise your colleague with happy words and gestures on getting a promotion. Do you feel real happiness or say that he/she might have used some evil way to get the promotion?

You talk to the beautiful opposite gender younger than you for half of your age. You stare below the neck, on turning, watch from the back, analyze the art of God for creation in the right or wrong proportion?

You watch every single thought of yours for a week and then observe whether your words and actions match or mismatch. I hope you could write me an email mentioning how and when you got understanding and agree with my comments.

The peak of irony is that your wife's fire is still burning. She needs you now, but you are helpless. Biologically you are vulnerable, and mentally you cannot penetrate.

Do you have any idea that during the same age, what is going on with your wife? Mother Nature takes the gift of fertility back from your wife in her fifties. (Age may vary with a person). She is under her menopause. There is a huge hormonal change she is suffering along with mental stigma and fatigue to suffer. Physically she has to suffer a lot. She has rage, depression, and happiness due to hormonal imbalance in her brain and body. She needs you badly at this phase of her life.

Do you support her?

I don't know, ask yourself.

My point is you do not care about your wife. There is a need for much care and attention from you to your wife. If you could focus all your thoughts on your wife, it will be great at your end to show gratitude to your wife. Till now and till her last breath, she will support you. It would be better if you take care of her. You must, "Love Your Wife."

The time frame in which you are living your life is crucial. By the time you will cross thirty years of your marriage, your kids are into their professional life. There is a small possibility that your kids are planning their nuptials. Either you arrange or organize the marriage ceremonies of your kids by this age of yours.

To support my thoughts, I wish to mention a theory of Indian Philosophy from ancient scriptures:
Ashrama in Hinduism is one of four age-based life stages discussed in Indian texts of the ancient and medieval eras. The four ashramas are:

1. **Brahmacharya (Student):** Brahmacharya (up to the age of 24 years) represents the student stage of life. This stage focuses on education and includes the practice of celibacy. The student must acquire knowledge of science, philosophy, scriptures, and logic, practice self-discipline, and learn to live a life of dharma - righteousness, morals, and duties.

2. **Grihastha (Householder):** This stage (from the age of 24 to 48 years) referred to the individual's married life, with the duties of maintaining a household, raising a family, educating one's children, and leading a family-centered and a dharmic social life. Grihastha stage was considered as the most important of all stages in a sociological context. As human beings in this stage not only pursued a virtuous life, they produce food and wealth that sustain

people in other stages of life, as well as the offsprings that continue humankind. The stage also represents one where the most intense physical, emotional, occupational, social, and material attachments exist in a human being's life.

3. Vanaprastha (Retired): The retirement stage (from 48 to 72 years), where a person hands over household responsibilities to the next generation, takes an advisory role, and gradually withdraws from the world. Vanaprastha stage is a transition phase from a householder's life with greater emphasis to be shifted from Artha and Kama (wealth, security, pleasure, and desires) to one with a greater focus on Moksha (spiritual liberation).

4. Sannyasa (Renunciation): The stage (from 72 plus years) is marked by the renunciation of material desires and prejudices, represented by a state of disinterest and detachment from earthly life, generally without any meaningful property or home(Ascetic), and focuses on Moksha (salvation), peace and simple spiritual life. Anyone can enter this stage after completing the Brahmacharya stage of life.

The Ashram system is one facet of the Dharma concept in Hinduism. It is also a component of the ethical theories in Indian philosophy. It is combined with four reasonable human life goals (Purusartha) to fulfill happiness and spiritual liberation. Moreover, since the four ashramas can be seen as the framework of an influential life-span model, they are also part of indigenous developmental psychology, which has shaped many people's orientations and goals from its ancient beginnings until today, especially in India.

Why have I referred to the four parts of life span as per spiritual teachings?

If you follow the same in your life, your life will be beautiful, and you will live in the present. As per the theory, you are on the verge of entering into the vanaprastha ashram in your life.

Do you feel you are ready to enter the third stage of your life, where you can live in this materialistic world, untouched?

The state of mind is achievable while living in a materialistic world.

Believe me! I have achieved this state of mind at the age of forty-four.

Phase Thirteen
FORTY Years of Your Married Life

"There is no more lovely, friendly, and charming relationship, communion, or company than a good marriage."

- Martin Luther

The decade of forty years!!

Forty years is a mammoth life span in your married life. In a fictional way, today's young generation will think that some characters stayed together with one spouse for forty years. Great times passed!!

Today's youth want everything instant. Life has become an instant recipe. They want fast food to eat. They want the food to get digested in no time. They want to become super-rich and superstars overnight. They want to grab the knowledge of the world by watching a five to fifteen-minute video. Youth do not want to read a book; they want to listen to audiobooks. The world is moving forward with the instant recipe. The way the Doraemon cartoon shows Doraemon's gadgets, it takes out from the belly pocket a colossal door and enters into any time and space. How beautiful a concept to think of, and if ever it is real? WOW!!

Have you seen Steve Rogers Transformation Scene - Captain America: The First Avenger (2011) Movie? A soldier of the

American army put in a machine, and in some time, a human becomes superhuman. The flat chest gets converted into a massive chest and six-packs with incredible power and capacity to fly. (https://www.youtube.com/watch?v=F020aNi0wS0) Again, WOW!!

Today's youth want it the same way. They wish that they will take a slumber, and once they wake up, the world is at their feet. They are at the top of the world. Where has the world reached? The world has gone from marriages to divorce and what not! What Next?

Further, youth may want an instant child.

Think!

You are admitted to a hospital. The doctor will inject an I.V. medicine into you and your wife. You wait for one hour. Spray the three hundred million sperm. Come out in one hour. Wait outside the room overnight. A team of doctors is working overnight with your wife with various machines. Morning at six O'clock, you get the baby in your hand. MY! MY!

You are laughing at this imagination. Wait for a hundred or some more years, and this will be the reality of life. I am fully confident and have trust in medical science, quantum physics, microbiologists, organic chemistry, biotechnologists, and artificial intelligence experts, with the help of the Japanese supercomputer, Fugaku (the latest and smartest of the league), the team, with their combined efforts, will achieve what I am visualizing today. Hundred Years from now, your grandchildren will laugh at you that you have wasted nine precious months of your life in the mother's womb. They took birth in nine hours. Not able to believe it. No issues!!

THINK.

- The generation before the Wright brothers, did it believe in man flying in the sky?   NO.
- One hundred and fifty years old generation, did it believe that the whole city could be on death in seconds?   NO.
- One hundred years old generation, did it believe that man will reach Mars?   NO.
- Did Alexander have the astounding belief that he does not require traveling a country to conquer? He just needed to give in order, SHOOT, and; the country could be eradicated.   NO.

History is full of examples. As Suggested by 'Daniel Goleman' in his best-in-class book on the topic, you need to pay **"focused attention."** How can I expect you to believe in me? It's completely okay. All the people who took birth up to this year 2020 have rare chances to experience the truth of my statement of birth of a child in nine hours. Simultaneously, the humans (maybe robots, clones, and aliens too) who will read my book in the year 2120 will unquestionably believe and get the chance to experience the same. They will praise me for my thoughts. I am excited for the same. Suppose you are reading this book in the year 2120 and praising my thoughts. Kindly accept my heartfelt gratitude and thanks from my end as I am not alive in the physical body. Still, my words are there for you to exhilarate.

I am writing a book in the year 2020. We must talk back about today. You have traveled long on a bumpy road of your life. The road gave you some serene experiences of life where you must have enjoyed bold and beautiful pleasure. The road bumps must have brought the opportunity to experience the best and worst ever incidents in life. Still, you came over everything as a winner. You are conquering since your marriage, don't you? The decade of thirty to forty years of married life is a decade of eternal experiences. **HOW?**

You and your wife are running in the age of sixties. Before this age, some various exciting changes and developments took place in this life. The changes were on the emotional and physical level. Some experiences of the change you got in your life remained permanent, and some for a while. I will explain to you how.

In the second year of your life after birth, you have learned to speak about your surroundings' mother tongue and other languages. You cannot become dumb in your life after that except the medical reason. Learning a language is a permanent change. You grew up from your childhood and reached adulthood. You cannot attain childhood again, which you desperately want at times. Enjoying childhood is a temporary phase of your life.

Similarly, during the peak of your youth, your adulthood, the perennial source of energy you enjoyed, was temporary. The power is exhausted by you. The enjoyment and the use of energy, enthusiasm, excitement, vitality, and endurance were all temporary. It has gone from your life now. Simultaneously, the change in color of your hair, skin tone, wrinkles on your face and neck (visible) is permanent with you. In your youth, you have worked for eighteen, sometimes twenty hours a day. You need to rest now. You cannot handle that long. Your speed in any work has gone worse. You take a longer time to accomplish every piece of work.

Here comes the role of love. Your wife helps you with everything. The painkillers, ointments, and oils have replaced the fragrance of excellent deodorant and ecstatic perfumes. God forbid! You may be suffering from knee pain, frozen shoulder, beginning of the varicose vans, diabetes, blood pressure, cholesterol, asthma, allergy to various items, and so on. Your wife takes charge of everything;

no outside partner will help and support you after thirty years of your marriage. The soap bubble of external attraction blows away from your life. Your wife is the only hope. You have no control over your impulses, so you cannot bear the pain due to any kind of ailment in your life. You lie down on the bed, dependent on your wife. She takes care of everything along with her illnesses.

Your grandchildren are approaching their teenage years and watching you and your children closely. Your grandchildren closely monitor your behavior towards your wife and your children. In the digital age of 2020, if a child cries after birth, parents show a cartoon or rhyming video. If you misunderstand that your grandchild has no intellect to identify your mood swings and behavioral patterns, then you are mistaken. I must say you are making another blunder. YOU MUST WATCH YOUR WORDS AND ACTIONS.

The best way is to remain the same, always. Become a cool, calm person. Leave your frustration of lost energy. Come out of the depression that you are not able to stand on Everest anymore. Even the supplements are helpless. Accept the fact that you have enjoyed your life to the fullest. Love your wife in a way that genuinely you are showing gratitude to her for all the pains she took in life for you.

STOP irritating on small and silly issues on your wife, children, and grandchildren. STOP scolding everyone around to guide you as per your experience. The world has changed. The youth has got the newest likings. Accept that the world is moving toward LGBT. You are not a part of it so leave it. In any case, you will not be alive to experience the repercussion of LGBT in the next thirty years. Why do I worry about the same? You may feel that the world around you is deteriorating. Agree. Can you help it? NO.

Then why to worry and spoil the surroundings? Mother Nature has its ways to balance the planet and its atmosphere. You don't need to worry. You are about to reach towards your retirement or might be already retired. Enjoy your retirement life with your wife. Accept the truth that after retirement, you are a fused bulb. Don't understand the theory? I will explain it to you.

Suppose someone reaches up to the highest administrative post in any government department or up to the private job's top-level positions. You may be the head of any of the various departments in any country. You may or may not have earned a lot of respect. You may or may not be highly educated. You may or may not have got housemaids, chaffers, etc. You may or may not be the owner of various luxury vehicles.

The moment you retire, the respect and benefits you were getting on the high post are also withdrawn. The world has respect for the chair and not for the human. People who understand this theory well are the happiest people after retirement. It doesn't matter if you are a bulb of 0, 5, 10, 40, 100, 200 watts, LED, halogen, fluorescent bulb, or any latest type. Once you are fused, you are fused. That's all you need to understand. What do you do with a fused bulb at home? You throw the bulb in the dustbin or show a way to the storeroom so as applied to you. The materialistic world of today sees from the eyes of earning. The moment you stop making it in your life, you are retired. You are a fused bulb. You have to learn to manage yourself in the storeroom if not in the dustbin. Your wife is the only hope. There are possibilities that some of your friends or colleagues might have departed for their heavenly abode, who could be psychological support to you.

Suppose you wish to live a happy life, then you have one good option along with many, **"Love Your Wife."**

Phase Fourteen
FIFTY Years of Your Married Life

"Love is something eternal-the aspect may change, but not the essence."
- Vincent van Gogh

My God!

You are alive and crossed forty years of your married life. What an achievement? You are a tough guy. You must have energy reservoirs and utilize them in a way that could support you to dwell. Congratulations!!

You are retired now. Suppose living happily. Then God must love you. Suppose you cannot live happily and then learn to live; otherwise, the remaining years of your life will be hell before reality.

You are replacing your extended life visits of luxury bars, five to seven-star hotels and restaurants, spa, pub, casino, etc., with specialized doctors, luxury hospitals, physiotherapy centers, pathology labs, MRI centers, etc.

The decade of forty to fifty years of your married life is crucial in various terms. You may arrange for or attend the marriage of your grandchildren. One of you or both of you might depart for your heavenly abode. There is a possibility that by now, your flight may take off. It depends on your lifestyle. Do you have any idea about this flight? You may or may not understand. I will explain it to you.

This planet is the airport of the almighty. God has created a system of a flight's landing and takeoff. The moment you were born out of your mother's womb was your landing moment on this planet's airport. The moment you are breathless is the takeoff moment of your life from the airport. Every second in the world, many flights are landing, and many are taking off. God's system is flawless. God has installed perfect artificial intelligence software for making all these arrangements. Each one of us is a visitor on this planet. I being a spiritual disciple, can elaborate this much as per my understanding. You may find religious gurus to understand it deeply. I believe in this theory. You may or may not. We all must respect each other's viewpoints in this world to live in harmonious ways. I respect you. You take your call.

Some of us may have the fire still burning beneath the ashes. That keeps you warm. It's acceptable, as it is God's system to make you wait till the time your flight takes off. You may be enjoying the serene atmosphere of home or surrounded by beautiful, expert, active, energetic nurses in the hospital. This stage of life brings you naked in front of doctors and nurses, as the case may be. In youth, you did it with your choice. Destiny also has its plans. You are often unconscious under anesthesia and unaware of what the hell is being done with your body by doctors and nurses.

Doctors and nurses are experts in their work. They cut you in, in such a way that as per the plans of God, you should be able to wait till your flight takes off. Your entire ego, proud of having a substantial king-size life, has no value. The doctors and nurses know very well that all kings are of the same size lying on the hospital table, and there is no difference.

Believe me, once you have got this understanding about life, life becomes easy. The sooner you understand, the better you start living in the present. I understood with a deep intensity that I live only in the present and visualize the future but never worry. I am ready to depart from the planet if God has plans though I have spent only seventeen years of my married life. It is all the same, always seventeen or seventy-one; it doesn't matter. It is your attitude to look at things.

You are well aware that anytime the announcement will be there for your departure. Still, you are busy making the world act as per your instructions. You want your wife to listen. I am mentioning the wife and not the number. The wife of any number, be it first, second, third, or more, doesn't matter. Your age is essential. At the age of seventy plus, you want to instruct. You wish that your wife must get up the moment you order. She should eat what you eat. She should rest when you rest. She should have the energy which she possessed after marriage. Probably you feel that the age of your wife is not advancing. Kindly do not compare your wife with your daughter-in-law. At the same time, do not compare your daughter-in-law with your wife's young age after your marriage. Time has changed. The water has flown away a lot. Your daughter-in-law's likes and dislikes and the habits of your wife cannot match in any case.

I put my example. I am working as a school principal and having a job role in instructing personnel to handle the school. Currently, I am forty-five, but after seventy, if I remain alive and demand my surroundings the way I was doing before my enlightened state, I will be the biggest fool. I am not going to do that, as I am not doing it even today. I am living in the present. I have accepted that if I leave my Principal's chair even today, I will be a fused bulb for this job role. It is the reason I do all my work in school myself-no peon opens the door for me. No peons carries my belongings. I dust my table if required. I first say happy morning to my staff, including the fourth class. I have stopped expecting anything from anyone. I have learned very well that whatever I want in my life, I have to give it first. I respect my teachers, staff, students, and parents. Suppose as a human, yes, I am a human and can achieve the same state. So you too can do it, provided you are a human.

What is the point of reference here? The matter of concern here is that your wife took a lot of pain in her life for you. Let her live her life as she is also moving ahead. Still, you are bothering her a lot. You want to show your supremacy over your wife. In reality, she is the only person in the world who listens to you. Rest. No one is listening to you.

Why?

You have not learned to control any of your emotions in life till now. Give one chance to yourself to improve your performance, stand before God. God is a relentless examiner. There are no chances of emotional drama in front of him. If you are failing, you are failing in the eyes of God. God has no biases. God never discriminates among any of us. Whatever numbers of flights are landing every second, they all are the same. It is we who are creating discrimination on the planet. We make the class, the cast, the creed, the color, the clan, the community, and all discriminations.

In school, I always find some students in higher classes who never study throughout the year. They learn a month before the exams. They enjoy the whole year by hanging out with friends, partying, watching movies, spending time on social media, gossiping and making fun of their teachers, and so on so forth. A month before exams, they come in action mode. They get up at two a.m., or they stay awake till two a.m. They respectfully talk to teachers, collect

Soumitra Singh Thakur

notes, practice questions, solve mathematical problems. What is the result of their efforts?

They get comparatively good grades. They cannot stand with the toppers, I agree. They are also not standing with the bottom ten. They are happy with their performance. Their parents keeping the students routine throughout the year are far more delighted with the performance.

You also have this chance to improve your performance in front of God. I agree you cannot top. You can have a fair result. I have understood the study's value and targeting the remaining six months of my lifespan in examining life. I have improved my performance tremendously. God says to learn to live in the present through the ancient scriptures, self-help authors, religious books, saints, priests, and Sadguru rest everything I (God) will take care of. So! Ask yourself, "Have I learned very well to remain in the present?" You have a fair chance even now in your hand to live in the present. Once you cross this phase and suppose your wife's flight takes off before you, and then you have nothing in your hand. Nothing in your hand will remain. Her flight takeoff first is a rare chance, but yes, chance is there.

You may ask, WHY?

She rarely smokes, drank her whole life. She controls her hunger and does physical activity throughout her life to manage the home and work balance. Her endurance is far better than you. There are rare chances that she takes off before you.

It is a suggestion that you respect and love your wife at this phase of your life. I love my wife every day, thinking that; tomorrow I may not be there to watch the sunrise, and my flight may take off before that. I cannot come back by making emotional tantrums to God to regret that I want to love my wife as I did not do in my whole life.

"If you did not love your wife for forty-plus years of your married life, then it is no point asking God to give you four days even to love your wife."

Do it today. Love your wife with the depth of your heart.

Show her gratitude for all those pains which she took in her life for you and your family. Talk to her relatives genuinely. You cannot rectify the errors. Stop making new errors. She will be happy the moment you start loving her-no question of physical love probably impossible for most men. Exceptional cases might be there. More than this, you are not even in the position to bear the luxuries as per your physical strength. The use of supplements with an overdose may trigger your flight to take off immediately. That could be fatal at your end. Take your own risk in case if you wish to.

My concern of love is to stop instructing her. Stop guiding, controlling, humiliating, or letting her down. Say her 'Thank You' for her emotional immolation for you in this life. Show gratitude for her efforts to make your house heaven. Show appreciation to provide the right education to your children. Say her "I Love You" for fulfilling all your fantasies your whole life in bed. Feel sorry (not by words, but in your inner world) to go around with chocolates and take a bite now and then during your youth (if applied to you).

Suppose you are not a spiritual practitioner in the real sense by this age, then you can do two tasks at this point of your life. First, love your wife. Second, retrospect on your life. There are fantabulous moments in your life since your first phase of preparing to get married till now. Recollect those meaningful moments of life in your memory and spend time with your wife. Till now, if you would not have spent time with her, or due to any reason if you have not enjoyed the morning tea or your meal, then do it. If possible, try to cook a dish of her choice for her. Whole life, she took your care; now it's your turn. Offer her a cup of tea daily. Take care of medicines which she requires and provides her on time. Sit and spend time with her. Speak to your children along with her. Have a video call with your kids and relatives along with her and enjoy life. Love your wife.

Phase Fifteen
You Alone in Your Married Life

"There is a remarkable difference between solitude and loneliness. Being alone isn't the worst feeling in the world, but being lonely is."

- Anonymous

My My!

You have crossed fifty years of your married life. You must be somewhere around your eighties. May God let your wife and you, both together, celebrate the fiftieth anniversary, the Golden Jubilee of your marriage. Suppose celebrated together along with your great-grandchildren, and it's incredible, man.

This chapter of the book is focused on you alone in your married life. I regret the sad demise of your loving wife. It is the destiny of every one of us. No one, NO ONE, can live forever. Everyone has to leave one day and that too alone without any article of the materialistic world.

I wish to mention Alexander the Great's last words and his last three wishes on the deathbed for all of us to learn lesson.
Alexander, while returning home after conquering many kingdoms, fell mortally ill in Babylon. While lying on his deathbed in the palace of Nebuchadnezzar (neh·byoo·kuhd·neh·zuh) II, he realized the worthlessness of his vast hoard of gold, silver, and

147

jewels, accumulated through his conquests with his sharp sword and his mighty army. He called his generals and said, "I will depart from this world soon. I have three wishes; please carry them out without fail." "I would like the world to know of three fundamentals through my last wishes:

"My first wish is that my physicians alone must carry my coffin," said Alexander.

I want my physicians to carry my coffin because people should realize that no doctor can cure anybody. They are powerless and cannot save a person from the clutches of death.

"My second wish is; I want the path leading to my grave to be strewn with gold, silver, and precious stones which are in my treasury while my body is being carried to be buried.

My second wish to strew gold, silver, and other precious stones on the way to the graveyard is to let the people know that though I spent all my life accumulating riches, not even a grain of gold will come with me when I leave this world. I want people to understand that it is a sheer waste of time, energy, and peace of mind when one yearns to be rich.

The dying king continued,

"My third and last wish is that both my hands be kept dangling out of my coffin."

With my third wish of having my hands dangling out of the coffin, I want people to know that I came empty-handed into this world and likewise will go empty-handed from this world."

"Bury my body, do not build any monument, keep my hands outside so that the world knows the person who won the world had nothing in his hands when dying."

- Last words of Alexander the Great.

What is the point?

The point is no one can carry even a dust particle in the last flight of departure from this planet. The irony is that everyone keeps on collecting a heap of money and worldly articles their whole life. Though it has been you; who did not give your wife, kids, and family time in your entire life and claim whatever I am doing, I am doing it for all of you. They wanted your time and love. You gave them money and materialistic items.

History is full of forts, empires, emperors, and the world's wealthiest people. You know it, watch, read, and talk about everything. The crucial point is you never follow it. It matters a lot that you didn't give time to your wife, kids, and parents. You kept on collecting big money. It is a probability that you are sitting in a colossal bungalow or a small house reading the book. In any case, you are alone. Your kids have left you for their bread and butter, and your wife is resting in peace. You are alone today.

Have you thought of ever?

What have you achieved in life? For what purpose you worked so hard to earn money. Why have you always controlled your wife and kids and fell into a quarrelsome situation on silly and trivial issues? Why have you raised your voice on various topics? Why did you have a habit of scolding? Did you gain something other than regret in your life?

I agree that there are people out in the world who love their wives a lot. They remain with the same spouse in their whole married life in the real sense; they do have earnings in their life. They are also alone in this phase of life. They have cherished memories; they have a huge friend circle to hang around even at this age. The true lover of his wife is a man who has been respected by everyone worldwide. Their family is full of members. Their family stays with them even if the wife is resting in peace. They spread happiness. The fragrance of their presence is easily identifiable by anyone. People love their company. They give positive vibrations to everyone surrounding them. Youth want to talk to them and wish to take benefit of their experience. They guide and mentor everyone who approaches them.

How are they able to do it?

They have learned to live in the present, and so do I. Till now, these lovers lived in the present and continue the practice. They are the happiest humans on the earth. They have no regrets. The "Field of Potentiality" (FP) explained by PAM GROUT in her beautiful book E2 works for them realistically. The FP works for everyone. One who loves his wife and the other who does not; both benefit from FP as per their acts.

Positive will attract positive, and negative will attract negative. What do you want back in your life? Use the FP for your benefit; it is available for everyone. So what are you thinking? Get up and start the best use of FP for the rest of your life. Still, one paper is remaining for your final examinations of life to get over. Use it well to improve your grades, so that next life (If ever it exists in your opinion) would be far better.

Else

You are alone in your massive or small house, wandering here and there. Have no goal, objective of what to do. You have not learned to cook your food. You don't know how to wash clothes. You don't know how to keep clothes in the closet. Whole life, you depended on your wife and that too, with a volley of scolding and abusive words. There is a possibility you are in the nursing home, as your children might send you and live in the house which you constructed working day in and day out your whole life. Another possibility is there that you are in the hospital. Eyes have blurred vision. Cataract could be the reason. The needles piercing your body in a day are the rewards of your abusive words and thoughts, which you played within your whole life. The doses of insulin via injecting the medicine are what; it is the system of rewards by God to you by your hands. You pierce your body with needles and punish yourself. Still, you don't understand the theory of Heaven and Hell. You are living in Hell.

There is no Heaven or Hell above the planet anywhere. It was a theory inscribed by early humans to make everyone understand the way of living. You did not learn yet. Did you meet any person alive who claims that he had seen heaven?

I DID NOT. TAKE YOUR CALL.

Many of you want to meet angels in heaven. They will do many things with you as per your fantasies. You want to go early. What will you do if you cannot carry your king-size earnings as the great king Alexander couldn't carry a single dust particle? The enjoyment of standing on Everest, which you experienced throughout life, the same Everest couldn't be felt ever again. What is the use then for this longing to go in heaven and meet Angeles? In any case, if this is true that you will get angels in heaven, then you must get a new body, the vast and mammoth Everest of heaven. Then why worry about the current?

Suppose you meet all the faithful saints and spiritual gurus in the world; they will tell you the Heaven and Hell are here on the earth, and it occurs only in your lifetime. I clarify it with my understanding of Heaven and Hell on earth and believe me, I live in paradise. I start with Hell first and end with Heaven to give you a lasting impression of thoughts in your mind.

Hell on earth during your lifespan: The creation of Hell emotionally starts from the teenage of humans. To understand in a better way, I am putting a few emotions here.

Fear: You are fearful of various things. You are afraid of darkness, height, water, vehicle, airplane, hospital, blood, and many more things in life. You always worry about natural calamities. You are worried about earthquakes, volcanoes, thunderstorms, accidents, cancer, and deaths around you. **This is Hell.**

Anger: You are angry at everyone surrounding you. You may be a student, fresher, bachelor, married, employee, employer, subordinate, manager, boss, owner, leader, neighbor, or anyone. You are angry about silly things. You are a crimson red hotplate. The moment water droplets fall on you, you react. Everyone surrounding you is fearful of you for your behavior. Kids are reluctant to come near to you. You are angry with your wife, kids, and family, and they ignore and avoid your presence. **This is Hell.**

Sadness: You are sad about the small changes in your life. Your regular salary credit date is 5th, and today is 6th. Salary is not credited. You are sad. You have applied to switch the job and not getting a call, you are unhappy. You have got a mild headache or fever; you are down. **This is Hell.**

Soumitra Singh Thakur

Jealousy: You are a jealous person. You have a colleague who has got a drive with a beautiful fresher, and you are jealous. Anyone who does any act in your surroundings remains happy with other people's growth and happiness. You keep on worrying about their development and use slang and abusive words for them internally. You always vibrate negatively to the person who shows growth for anything. Same you get in return. **This is Hell.**

Disgust: You see a heap of garbage while traveling, you feel disgusted. You come across a bagger or a poor person, or you get along with a disabled person, you feel disgusted. While walking, someone mistakenly throws garbage on you, you feel disgusted and rebuke. **This is Hell.**

Problem: You are a problem, man. You have a problem with children, parents, humans, society, politics, NGOs, social media, newspapers, politicians, businesspersons, traders, vendors, relatives, friends, wife and the list is infinite. Whatsoever happens around you, you have a problem. Sometimes you have a question with Mother Nature why is there a sudden rainfall, snowfall, or no fall. **This is Hell.**

A comprehensive list is infinite with me to explain the Hell in your life. I am concluding it with one last point.

Illness: The illness in your life is also a type of Hell experience for you. You have various kinds of pains in the body at different times; they are acute pain, chronic pain, neuropathic pain, nociceptive pain, and radicular pain. My point is every pain is the experience of presence in Hell. All the disease counting from blood pressure, thyroid, diabetes, AIDS, cancer, burn, fracture, or any medical term is an experience of Hell on the earth. Even acidity on a day to day basis is belonging to the same experience. **This is Hell.**

Heaven on earth during your lifespan: God has bestowed us heaven after our birth as a reward. We all experience heaven in our lives but forget to maintain it.

Have you ever thought of why you have a sheer urge to become a child in your depression state or sadness? Children up to five years of age are living in heaven on earth. They do not have fear. You throw a small child in the air and catch him/her, and he will smile at you.

- A child never raises his voice or scolds anyone. The child knows no anger.

- A child can play with a heap of garbage and in the mud. The child knows no disgust.

- A child gets happy with the toy of another child and plays. The child knows no jealousy.

- A child has no problem with anyone in the world. The child is happy for others.

- A child loves everyone unconditionally. A child is the happiest human on the earth. Why? It is because a child lives in the present. **This is Heaven.**

Heaven on earth is achievable. If you are fearless, you are free from anger, free from jealousy, and love; unconditionally. It is an abstract state of achievement, and I have achieved it in my life.

You can live in heaven on earth. You will love your wife, your kids, and your parents. Like me, people around you respect you, praise you, and seek guidance from you. You will know no anger, no jealousy, no disgust, no sadness, no fear of failure, no worries of the past, and no worries of the future. You will never complain, never blame, never pull anyone's leg and have fewer medical issues. You will have only positive things around you. Your dear ones will always be happy with you. People around you will not be reluctant about your presence. They would like to spend maximum time with you to seek help or guidance. No one will ignore you. Everyone who knows you will be ready to take your phone calls even after many years of disconnection.

What else could be the definition of Heaven on earth?

Your words and actions will match. You will say, "I am living in heaven."

I am saying this to you as I am leading such a wonderful life of positivity and hopefulness. I have achieved it all in my life; for this achievement, I am grateful to my spiritual guru, family, and friends and, above all, to the omnipotent forever.

I have heartfelt gratitude for you to be an avid reader of my book. I am thankful that my book is in your hands, a human with an intelligent brain and a beautiful heart like you. I am grateful that my book got a reader knowledgeable of your level to read my thoughts in the form of words. I am pleased that you are keeping a paperback copy for your future reference in case of need. I would be the happiest and most grateful person on the earth if I ever get a chance to read the opinion and feedback of a human who is so intelligent and as knowledgeable as an encyclopedia, in the form of an email on my email address: i.e., connect@soumitrathakur.com.

May God Bless You with Heaven on the earth and ahead of this planet!!

Soumitra Singh Thakur

Practical Suggestions for a Joyous Married Life

The reality is that ample theoretical knowledge is available on the internet, in books, and with saints. Each one of us knows and is aware of life situations, problems, and solutions. Whatever I wrote in the book is in a different proportion known to everyone. This concept of knowledge is like Sun-Light.

I am confident; that I wrote this book in the style of a **self-talk** book. The benefit of self-talk is that there is no worry about people's judgment. No one raises a finger on you when you are talking to yourself. You know all your secrets, mistakes, and inner thoughts. You are naked in front of you, and you have no worries. You are not ashamed of your nakedness as no one comes to know about it.

If you analyze a wrong step or a mistake, the benefit of self-talk is that you have a chance to take the right action or rectify the error. You can guide, instruct, and order to yourself. The moment you have self-talk and get ready to implement the self-talk suggestions:

YOUR EGO DOES NOT STOP YOU TO TAKE ANY RECTIFYING STEP.

Suppose I offer you practical suggestions; you may say a big "NO" to it, **Like:**

- **Get-up before Sunrise.**   NO.

- Drink water after getting up.   NO.

- Have bodily exercise.   NO.

- Stop eating fast food.   NO.

- Stop drinking cold drinks.   NO.

- Be Humble.   NO.

- Be Honest.   NO.

- Remain cool and calm.   NO.

- Quit smoking.   NO.

- Quit taking alcohol.   NO.

I am sure, by this time, you have understood my viewpoint, now:

HAVE A SELF-TALK. LOOK YOURSELF NAKED IN YOUR MIND MIRROR AND SEEK SUGGESTIONS FROM YOUR OWNSELF.

Revise your secrets. Ask questions to yourself and move into action.

Capitulate; your anger, ego, attitude, lust, jealousy, and hate, etc., to God.

All these belong to you.

Rest all belongs to god, and god provided you for the use of this life.

Be grateful to God for providing you this beautiful life on this planet.

Show gratitude to your parents to be a part of giving life to you on this planet.

Touch your mother's feet daily for bearing a lot of pain to give you life on this planet.

Show gratitude and say "I Love You" to your first wife (If you have) to take a bold step of marrying you to bear all the life pains to provide you pleasures on this planet in life.

You must say thank you and show your gratitude to the people who have brought happiness to your life.

You must forgive those who hurt you at times in your life.

You must make apologies from the depth of your heart with the people to whom you did wrong.

I am sure God will help you. The field of potentiality will help you.

My workable and doable suggestions are on a mental level, you can do it quickly, and no one knows about it. I am sure; when you follow your instinct, you follow it by heart, with genuineness; and it will work.

Keep applying, implementing, and following the indirect suggestions so that it is easy to start and stop without knowing anyone in the world other than you. You will enjoy living in the world the way you want to live. Last but not the least tip of joyous married life:

DO NOT INTERFERE IN THE EMOTIONAL SELF OF YOUR WIFE!

Live Life, King Size!! AND "Love Your Wife"!!

Acknowledgments. . .

Writing a book is building a castle. It takes time. This book is the outcome of learning of; forty years of my life. From the age of five years, whatever I have observed, learned from human relationships has got a place in this book's way of thoughts.

Suppose I wish to write the names of people who made me learn life lessons and gave me insight into understanding spirituality by being into the materialistic world. It needs to write another book of acknowledgments.

A heartfelt thanks and gratitude to every person who knows me personally, brought me up, played with me, studied with me, spent time with me at any point in my life since my childhood till this age, and will visit in my life; in the future.
A heartfelt thanks to all the teachers, coordinators, and my school owners & directors, with whom I worked in my long career at a different period in the education field.

A heartfelt thanks to all the parents of my students. Who came in contact during my long tenure as a principal and allowed me to observe and understand human behavior and enriched me with life experiences.

Still, there are a few names that I could mention here who contributed during the journey of making this book.
My loving brother-in-law Mr. Munish to be the constant advisor for the professional world.

My mentor in the teaching profession and first editor of this book, the motherly figure in my life Mrs. Nupoora Kulkarni. I owe you a lot in my life.

A special mention to *Mr. Ramchandra Hegde for supporting me during my stint in writing the book.*

A special thanks to Mr. Som Bathla for inspiring me to write a book. To identify the hidden talent of a writer in me.

Website designer and Mr. Sarvesh Kakkeri, a young and dynamic person.

The designer of the cover page, Mr. Akshay Ameria, Ujjain.

The digital media agency owner, Mrs. Khyati Agarwal, and her team.

The list is endless...

A sincere apology to any of the humans to whom I have hurt knowingly or unknowingly in my life span for a wanted, unwanted, personal, or professional reason.

Thank You For Being In My Life.

!! I Owe You All !!

Soumitra Singh Thakur

Who is Soumitra Singh Thakur?

Soumitra is a solemn educationist who spent twenty-one years, most as the principal educator, in India. He has transmuted into an enlightened soul and wrote his debut "Love Your Wife" as an author. He is an acclaimed academician with rich and qualitative experience from every walk of life and an observant of human behavior for several years to extract his students' best performances. He is a dynamic and enthusiastic leader-a very resourceful motivational speaker and a life trainer with a practical approach.

He is an Achievement-oriented professional with excellent people management skills and an ability to manage change with ease.

He has acquired excellent insight through his long career as an educationalist, highly effective administrator, a credential motivational rhetorician, and a corporate trainer for humans.

He is a highly motivated individual with excellent people and leadership skills and high educational ethics. He has built a consistently successful record of accomplishments in the academic field. His strengths and abilities have enabled him to work successfully with a variety of pupils and people.

He is a firm believer in **"Learn, Unlearn and Relearn"** for any individual to excel in Life.

Soumitra is working on a mission to build happy human relationships for people to live a harmonious life. He is a straightforward person with an inclination in spirituality, a meditator, and a yoga practitioner. He is the enlightened soul and learned to live in the present and remains untouched in the materialistic world.

He is a divergent and convergent thinker. He can distinctively and rapidly grasp the problem in an institute or individual. He can help them resolve it through his training and leading sessions supported by his skills. He has penned down his observations of Life in his debut, Love Your Wife, and is working on the next title, Love Your Husband, to bring happiness in the Life of two. Soumitra would be happy to help you resolve your hindrances to succeed on the path of becoming a happy human in Life. You can write Soumitra by putting your queries via **email connect@soumitrathakur.com,** and he will revert via his blog or podcast once you **subscribe to his blog.**

Soumitra calls you to dwell in the present to weave exhilarated succeeding days.

To get more insight about Soumitra and his work, visit **www.soumitrathakur.com.**